Are Wl Really Crabs in a BARREL?

The Truth and Other Insights About the African American Community

Dr. Rodney D. Smith

Copyright

Rodney D. Smith
Are WE Really Crabs in a BARREL: The Truth and Others Insights About the African American Community

Text and Cover Page copyright © 2016 by Rodney D. Smith
Self publishing

First Edition

ISBN 978-0-9975241-0-9

To Malcolm J. Smith

Contents

ACKNOWLEDGMENTS

I am deeply indebted to a number of people who have inspired this work and have richly contributed to my life. First among them are my wife and children. I thank God daily for the tremendous gift He has given me in them. To my wife, Stephenie K. Smith, you are the driving force of my life. You are, at once, my confidant, my sounding board, my advisor, my intellectual stimulus and my love. You inspire me to be. To my children, Phoenix and Chi, you sustain me. You are the reason God created me. You give my life direction and, most importantly, you give my life purpose. To my father and mother, Zeddie and Lillian Smith, you are the epitome of parenthood. Being your son has been and continues to be one of the greatest joys of my life. When I think of you, I am immediately reminded of the South African/Zulu term *Ubuntu*, which, loosely translated, means "I am because you are." To my brother, Eric C. Smith, you have always been in full support of everything that I do. You have been one of my biggest encouragers throughout my life. I will always look up to you for that. To my extended family and friends, your love has held me up. I feel it as I write these words.

To my role models and mentors during my formative years, you were "real life" examples of who I could become. You were all really smart and informed people, which communicated to me that I should and could be smart and informed too. It all started in the second grade with Mrs. Sumpter, a family friend whom I'm still in contact with today. It continued with my third grade teacher, Mrs. Atkinson, who was not only my teacher, but my neighbor and family friend as well. My fourth grade teacher was Mrs. Jefferson, who also happened to be married to the pastor of one of the most prominent African American churches in my hometown, Bethel A.M.E. Church. During my fifth grade year, I was fortunate to have three African American teachers. My school used a rotation model this particular year, so Mrs. Bibb, my homeroom teacher, also taught us Language Arts and Social Studies, and Mrs. Washington taught us Math and Science. Mrs. Washington was my neighbor as well. And not just any neighbor, but lived directed adjacent to me, and her husband, Mr. Danny, was my dad's good friend and co-worker. Our P.E. teacher was Ms. Gardner. She, too, was a family friend.

My transition to middle school was made a little easier because one of my six grade teachers was Mr. Herbert K. Knox. Mr. Knox was one of my dad's closest friends. I actually called him Uncle Herb, but not at school; I didn't want to blow our cover. In the seventh grade, Mr. Williams taught us Social Studies, and Mr. J. Green taught us Math. Mr. J. Green's brother, Mr. T. Green, also taught us that year, but I cannot remember what course he taught. In the eighth grade, Mrs. Bessilieu was my homeroom and English teacher, Mr. Pinckney, another family friend and neighbor, taught us Science. During middle school, we were exposed to a wide-array of vocational and extracurricular opportunities such as Carpentry, P.E. and the Marching Band. Our Carpentry/Wood Shop instructor was Mr. Nelson. Our P.E. instructor was Mr. Brown, and though I was not part of the Marching Band, Mr. Johnson, the Band Director taught an Introductory Music course. The Assistant Principal, Mr. Patterson, was a prominent member of the community and a member of the American Legion with my father.

My high school was structured such that our homeroom teacher would remain the same for the entire four year experience. I fortunately had Mr. Shubrick as my homeroom teacher. The Head Principal was Mr. Moultrie and Mr. Drayton was the Assistant Principal. Later, Mr. Lemmon and Ms. Rice became the Assistant Principals after Mr. Drayton retired. Mrs. L. Wragg was my ninth grade Algebra teacher and a distant relative. Mrs. L. Johnson was my ninth grade English teacher. Mrs. Doby was my tenth grade Biology teacher and my dad's high school classmate. Mr. Jones taught me Pre-Calculus during my senior year, and Mrs. Huell taught Intro to Accounting in my school's Career Center. There were several other African American teachers and administers who deeply impacted my life; some I never received direct classroom instruction from, but they influenced my life still the same. Mrs. Jones was a teacher and the mother of a dear friend. Mrs. Diggs was a Science teacher and the mother of another friend. Mrs. Chatman was the Office Administrator in the school's main office and served as everyone's mom away from home. Mrs. W. Wragg was a math teacher, a distant relative and Mrs. L. Wragg's sister. Mr. Nesmith was the instructor in the Automotive Repair Center, which was also part of the school's Career

Center. Mrs. Holmes and Mrs. Williams were the Guidance Counselors; Mrs. Holmes also happened to be my mom's really good friend and high school classmate. And, Mr. Kelly was a Science teacher and yet another neighbor.

Then there were my coaches. Coach Freddie Young, my Track and Field coach, is more than partially responsible for many of us going to college. He constantly harassed us about our college application processes and college entrance exams. There was also Coach Logan, Coach Barber, Coach Nelson (the same Mr. Nelson who taught Carpentry in middle school) and Coach Joey. They were all Assistant Coaches for the football team. And last but certainly not least, was Coach T. L. Smith.

I have saved him for last because, second to my father, Coach Smith has been the most influential man in my life. He actually coached my father some 30 years before he coached me. He was such the consummate coach, everyone referred to him as Coach, even if he never coached them. His wife even affectionately called him Coach. He was a legend in my hometown, and in many regards, I received the full benefit of all the years of his wisdom and knowledge. You see, I was the last Quarterback that he coached before he retired, and as a result, I was privy to every nugget of wisdom he ever possessed. Coach was an offensive mastermind who had been offered more than a few college coaching jobs but declined them all to stay and coach high school football. He was the kind of coach who instituted his own curfew for his players and drove around town after nightfall to enforce it. Coach and I had an extremely close relationship. He was far more than a football coach. All of his football strategies had life lessons woven into them. I find my

VII

self, even today, reciting many of his quotes and sayings. In fact, when I got to college, I joined Omega Psi Phi Fraternity, Inc. mainly because many of the gentlemen I have mentioned above, including Coach, were Omega men. I wanted to be like them. All of the individuals I have named were African American educators who helped to mold my life. They were tangible examples for me to emulate.

Finally, I would like to thank Dr. Whitney B. Edwards for her expert editorial eye during an early draft of this work, and Dr. Louis Woods for providing insightful comments and critiques from the beginning. I would also like to thank Mrs. Cynthia Fails for answering all my questions about getting published. You are gracious beyond measure. And certainly, this book would not have been possible without Mrs. Megan Cross, who served as my primary editor and writing consultant from start to finish. I thank you all greatly.

INTRODUCTION

"But if we had not loved each other, none of us would have survived."
James Baldwin

A few weeks ago, as I was about to board a flight, I overheard two African American young ladies discussing the possibilities of a job promotion. As we were being directed down the jetway, one of the young ladies was informing the other of her interest in applying for a director's position with her company. According to her calculations, she had been on the job long enough and was well-qualified to perform the tasks of the position. She planned to inquire about the job surreptitiously, because she did not want to fall prey to the "crabs in the barrel" mentality that ran rampant in her office. As she explained her thinking, she noted that she specifically wanted to steer clear of "the Black folk in the office." I spent the entire flight in deep thought about this commonly held belief that permeates the African American community.

We sometimes hear African Americans refer to other African Americans as crabs in a barrel. This metaphor is often used in an effort to describe the seemingly destructive behaviors of some Blacks toward other Blacks. An example of this phenomenon, for some, took place during President Barack Obama's initial presidential campaign in 2008, when many African Americans were peeved at the seemingly counterproductive actions of a few of the Black community's old guard[1] (e.g. Jesse Jackson, Andrew Young, Al Sharpton, etc.). These de facto leaders were accused of being crabs in a barrel when they did not initially support Obama's campaign efforts. In fact, in the early stages of the campaign, many were Hillary Clinton supporters for one reason or another. As a result, most of them were viewed as "haters" and, thus, characterized as crabs in a barrel. They were being accused of attempting to sabotage Obama's presidential aspirations.

During the 2012 presidential campaign, the crabs in a barrel analogy resurfaced in a major way because of the presidential aspirations of the GOP's only African American candidate, Herman Cain, and because of self-confessed support from individuals like Cosby Show alum, Joseph C. Phillips. Phillips, an African American actor and conservative commentator, has received considerable media coverage over the years because of his outspoken alliance with the Republican Party.[2] Cain's mere interest in the presidency as a GOP prospect and Phillips's unabashed support of conservative values were viewed as an affront to President Obama and caused many individuals to describe them both as crabs in a barrel.

Some may conclude that the aforementioned examples represent a fainthearted attempt on my part to defend the political views of the persons named above or that they symbolize my camouflaged declaration of an affiliation with the Republican Party. To the contrary, and in full disclosure, I have always favored liberal political principles throughout my life. I have referenced the scenarios above purely to illustrate the kinds of circumstances that sometimes spawn the crabs in a barrel analogy.

Though I have researched the metaphor rather extensively, I am not completely sure when it became common narrative in the Black community. I do, however, know from where the comparison comes. The metaphor derives from witnessing the behaviors of the marine life form commonly enjoyed on dinner tables throughout the world. I grew up in the small coastal town of Georgetown, South Carolina, and I gained quite a bit of experience dealing with these ten-tentacled sea creatures. I grew quite accustomed to seeing these crustaceans boiling in a large pot in preparation for dinner, mostly at a large family feast of some sort. It was always difficult to watch them boil, considering the fact that they were being cooked alive. Inevitably, one of the crabs would find a way to escape the boiling water and reach the rim of the pot. In most cases, another crab would grab the escaping crab and pull it back into the boiling water.

Without analytical thought, one may conclude that the arresting crab was attempting to sabotage the efforts of the escaping crab. On the surface, it appears that one crab is stopping the progress of another. If we were to analyze the situation a little deeper, we may conclude that the impeding crab is actually a desperate crab, grasping for survival. The challenge, though, is that the escaping crab has not yet securely anchored himself on the rim of the pot or on the outside of the pot. Thus, the desperate crab latches on too soon and pulls the escaping crab back down to his eventual death. If we follow this logic, it is quite understandable that a crab in boiling water would try to affix himself to an escaping mate in an effort to avoid certain death. The dilemma, however, is that the actions of one crab proves to be counterproductive to both crabs (and all of the other crabs in the pot, for that matter).

So comparatively, the correlation some African Americans make of other African Americans to crabs in a barrel may be unduly imparted or at least conferred out of context. We often compare ourselves to crabs without giving full consideration to either life form, humans or crabs. In the case of crabs, we must consider that crabs are not intended to live in barrels. Most thrive in vast bodies of water. And surely, they are not intended to live in pots of boiling water. We must acknowledge that the water is extremely hot and will result in death. Similarly, we must realize that the actions of some among us are often the result of despair. Many of our peers live under dire circumstances and act out of desperation. We must begin to question why so many African American families live under such dire circumstances. We must investigate the causes for so many Black folk living in poor neighborhoods, with very little opportunity for economic or educational growth. *(I will examine this thought a bit further in a subsequent chapter).*

By no means am I attempting to justify or excuse the actions of those in our communities who consciously hurt or cause harm to others. I am simply suggesting that we gain a better understanding of the circumstances, situations, and environments that many African American people find themselves in today.

On the other end of our conversation about Afri-

4

can American progress, we have had some people in our community, in their effort to claim their stake of America's promise, chase and capture the sometimes elusive dreams of meritocracy—a supposed system where progress is determined by an individual's talents and abilities. Their actions have been a good faith effort to blend into America's mainstream culture and play by the rules that ostensibly undergird the country. The results, for a select few, have been fruitful; they have successfully acquired a modicum of success. Many can now be classified as middle-class citizens. Unfortunately, the results for the majority have been fruitless, because the rules of progress and privilege are not always understood in an equitable way. Regrettably, we sometimes blame each other for these misfortunes, believing that our own have somehow sabotaged our progress. I have written this book in an effort to combat these beliefs and help us to see things differently. Like the author of the Book of Jude in the Bible who begins the text making clear his eagerness to write to his fellow man, and tells of his mandated duty to urge God's people to fight for their faith,[3] I too have been compelled by a Higher Power to urge my people through my writing to contend for the truth.

Among this book's many inspirations, I will mention, first, the young men of the inaugural class of the 100 KINGS Program in Nashville, Tennessee. They have inspired this work. I had the good fortune to serve as the Program's Director from 2003 to 2007 and in an advisory capacity between 2007 and 2010. The initiative was established to help a cohort of 100 fifth-grade African American male students matriculate through middle school, high school and on to college. The program's curriculum included training in personal growth and career selection, in addition to training in academic enrichment and college preparation. Training sessions were held on the campus of either of two major universities in Nashville on two Saturdays per month during the school year and six consecutive weeks during the summer months. Our relationships with the local universities helped to demystify the college experience and increased the students' expectations for higher education. Students received career mentoring from adult male mentors and academic tutoring from local college-aged mentors. Students expanded their worldviews and built leadership skills through hands-on service projects with local community organizations, including museums and fine arts establishments. Students were provided college scholarship support after successfully completing the program. The program also included financial literacy and parenting skills training for the students' parents.

This variety of personal, academic and social development activities were designed to help the students develop the knowledge, skills, confidence and network necessary for long-term success. Though I have always suspected that our indictment of crabs—and the humans who get compared to them—was inaccurate, the community effort it took for the 100 KINGS program to be successful helped to solidify my thoughts and feelings surrounding the phenomenon. The program was a complete community endeavor and, notably, most of the community members who assisted the program to success were African American. This fact runs counter to the popular tale about the African American community that says we are crabs in a barrel. I saw, firsthand, the community serving in opposition to the widespread narrative that African Americans, generally, are not supportive of each other. The young men and the community came together to create better lives for each other.

The young men of the program were the most impressive for the deep sense of community they developed among themselves. At the conclusion of the program, we held focus group discussions in an effort to assess how the program had impacted the participants' lives. We wanted to identify the parts of the program that initially piqued their interests, the ones that sustained their interests along the way and to identify the features that were most valuable to them overall. The students' comments and responses related heavily to their connections to each other, they said things like, "My brothers kept me interested in the program," "It was the bonds that were created that kept me interested in coming" and "The program was a brotherhood."

They walked away having gained one of the primary understandings that I, as the director, wanted them to possess. I wanted them to recognize a sense of accountability to each other. When we help our young men to understand that they are responsible for more than just themselves, we create better men, better husbands, better fathers and ultimately better communities. Coincidentally, one of our overarching mantras was, "I am my brother's keeper," which mirrors the title of an initiative President Obama and his administration launched in 2014. Hopefully, their sense of community and responsibility among each other does not stop within the brotherhood, but is extended to their larger community, and then their cities, states, and country. We can literally change the world by getting young Black males to understand their responsibilities outside of themselves.

My hometown of Georgetown, South Carolina was also an inspiration for this book. I draw specific inspiration from the many African American educators that impacted my life during my formative years. After a recent conversation with my second grade teacher, Mrs. Sumpter, I realize that I am now an educator because of all the wonderful educators I have had access to throughout my life. They planted this seed in me years ago, and this book is but a small indication that the seed has grown. I realize that many, if not most, African American students matriculate through 13 years of primary and secondary school without ever having the privilege of being taught by an African American educator. That definitely was not my experience. My experience with African American teachers started in the second grade with Mrs. Sumpter and has extended throughout my entire life.

The educators I make reference to above helped to shape my life. They were a part of an educated citizenry who, inadvertently, modeled for me specific possibilities for my life. I believe that our children will be what they see; I saw African Americans as smart and informed people, so I strived to be a smart and informed person. They were the antithesis to what we have come to characterize as crabs in a barrel.

Above all, this book has been written specifically to and for the African American community. As an African American educator and social scientist, I am most interested in the gaze of Black America. Thus, this piece has been written not to tear down any community, but to uplift my community. As you read through these pages, please do not interpret my telling of my view of America's past as a form of hate toward America. To the contrary, I love America and all who love the truth. My position is one of love. Simply because I love Black people does not mean that I hate others. Again, it is out of love that I have written this work. It is a love that incorporates and celebrates yesteryear—the good and the bad aspects of yesteryear.

You will notice that I use more than a few facts of history, not only as a backdrop to contemporary concerns, but as a key player in some of today's major impediments and obstacles. Though I am not a historian, I believe we are negligent if and when history is not considered as we attempt to address present-day circumstances. Even if history is recalled simply to remind us of how far we have come and how much we have endured, we must not forget the significance of our past. Again, I am not a historian; I am an educator, so I would be terribly remiss if I did not at least attempt to educate some and remind others about a few of the conditions that history has caused.

Finally, I write this book because I am now part of the Black middle-class that Dr. King admonished in his final manuscript, *Where Do We Go From Here*, to "rise up from its stool of indifference, to retreat from its flight into unreality and to bring its full resources—its heart, its mind and its checkbook—to the aid of the less fortunate brother."[4] Allow this work to stand as evidence that I am casting my heart, my mind and my resources with my less fortunate brothers and sisters. I have actually journeyed through the 5 Stages of Nigrescence (see Chapter 3) and have settled into an internalization of my identity. Along with this internalized identity has come a life-long commitment to my community, the Black Community.

Chapter Summaries

Chapter 1, "America's Founding," takes a serious look at how the country was founded and highlights some of the attributes that, I believe, created the wealthiest country the world has ever known. The chapter begins with an examination of slavery and the economic juggernaut it proved to be for America's financial stability. It specifically looks at the Mason-Dixon Line, the Northwest Ordinance, the U.S. Constitution and the Oceanic Slave Trade Ban of 1808 and focuses on how these American regulations combined to, for all intents and purposes, "quarantine" slavery to the Southeastern region of the country, which in turn caused interstate slave trade to spike. The chapter then turns to address some of the residual effects of slavery, particularly the less than ideal traits and behaviors that have lived on in Black communities. The chapter concludes with a discussion about some of the myths and misnomers that continue to plague Black America.

Chapter 2, "African American Males: Are We An Endangered Species," questions the so-called extinction of Black males. It starts by validating many of the reasons why some in society have suggested that the Black male is in danger of extinction. It highlights a few of the pitfalls that Black males are forced to traverse if and when we decide to live self-determining lives. Even though this chapter lays out many of the reasons why some have concluded that extinction is imminent, it vehemently takes a stance against even the remote possibility that African Americans males are an endangered species. This position is assumed because of the resiliency of the human spirit and species. More specifically, the chapter renders extinction improbable for Black males because of the Black community's undying faith in a Higher Power and in each other, and because of the community's record of endurance.

Chapter 3, "Measuring Success," confronts the country's criminal justice system and argues that it has operated largely on the backs of people of color. It makes the case that the image of crime has been hijacked by an unspoken bias and has been colored by preconceived notions. It also exposes the extremely powerful undercurrent of Whiteness in America and brings to light the *Cultural of Power* that is directed by the widespread ideologies of this concept of Whiteness. The chapter also hypothesizes about the identity development of African Americans in juxtaposition to other ethnic groups. The chapter then closes with full-on resistance to the resonating image of the *criminalblackman*.

Chapter 4, "Black Communities: Are They Poor and Destitute by Design?" interrogates past congressionally-sanctioned policies that systemically and systematically created poor communities in which people of color reside. The chapter specifically calls into question the schemes and tactics the banking industry employed following the Great Depression. It then transitions to the presidential policies of Franklin Delano Roosevelt and Harry S. Truman known as the New Deal and Fair Deal, respectively. The manner in which these policies were administered essentially exiled African Americans and other people of color from the benfits of these governmental programs. The chapter highlights this fact. It also argues that our past is more recent than we think. The chapter concludes by making a case to support and strengthen poor people. It pays special attention to how and why educating poor people is essential to America's overall success.

Chapter 5, "Conclusion: Now What?" encourages the Black community to take action in spite of the various structures that have been put in place to thwart our progress. It meticulously lays out several action items that will help African Americans to circumvent the so-called barrel. Principally, it encourages collaboration and collectivism. The chapter suggests that we are much better together than we are apart. It closes reiterating some of the historical and current facts that have created the proverbial barrel. Ultimately, it encourages African Americans to "get up, get out, and get something."

Again, *Are We Really Crabs in a Barrel* is devoted to the African American community. It is intended to inspire Black people to see themselves differently. It is also my hope to invoke and encourage a continued vigilance in the Black community. Vigilance is defined as "the state or quality of being keenly alert and watchful in order to detect danger." It was vigilance that sustained us through the pitch-black darkness of the Middle Passage. That same vigilance kept us safe when slavery tried to kill us. Vigilance was definitely the order of the day as we navigated the uncertainty of the Underground Railroad. Again, vigilance marched beside us as we erected the pillars of Civil Rights. And it will surely be vigilance that assists us as we discern the glimmers of future possibilities.

A Note on Racial Terminology

You will notice that I capitalize the terms "Black" and "White" throughout the entire book. There are some scholars who believe that the term "Black" should be capitalized, whereas the term "White" should remain in lowercase. They rationalize that "Black" or "African American" signifies a group that can only align themselves to an entire continent because their ancestry was disjointed as a result of slavery. And to the contrary, White Americans can trace their lineage back to various places, such as Ireland, Italy, Germany and so on. I understand their point, however, in an effort to be both equitable and respectful, I capitalize both terms. Similarly, I use the term "Latino" out of respect for my brothers and sisters of Latin American descent. Most of my Latino friends prefer the term instead of Hispanic.

Disclaimer

The content that you find here, I can assure you, is based on my understandings, and are the result of the way in which my sometimes non-sequential mind interprets concepts and situations. As such, a few passages, concepts and ideas that appear in this book have also appeared in some of my other writings (i.e. dissertation, book chapters, and blogs) as I have been grappling with many of the issues presented here for quite some time.

CHAPTER ONE
AMERICA'S FOUNDING

"My forefathers bled and suffered and died to create this
nation, and if my forefathers had not damned all those
rivers and picked all that cotton and laid all that track, there
would not be an American economy today."
James Baldwin

There is no denying the fact that past circumstances have directly affected modern-day conditions. It would be a bit myopic to believe otherwise. Much of the activities of yesterday determine outcomes for today's citizens. And certainly, African Americans are included in that citizenry. Any assessment that attempts to draw attention to the behaviors of Black folk, be it a comparison to crabs or not, must begin with an examination of America's history. For us to gain a better perspective on the lives that many African Americans lead today, we must take a hard look at this country's past. In particular, we must seriously and honestly examine

14

America's history of discrimination and marginalization. Any such examination must start at the country's founding.

We all know, quite well, the story behind the founding of America. Our grade school history textbooks did a good job of conveying the egalitarian idealisms that supposedly uphold America. As a result we have continuously attempted to persuade ourselves and others that our society was founded on genuine democratic values based on the laudable principles of justice and equality. Many sincerely believe that America's foundation provides equal opportunity for all and fosters meritocracy—a system where individuals are rewarded for their talent, capabilities and hard work. Though I acknowledge the progress this country has made over the years, America is no meritocracy. It never has been and has yet to truly reflect bona fide meritocratic principles. I understand that potential is universal in America, but unfortunately opportunity has not been. Sure, there are certain enclaves within our society that are nearing meritocracy, but overall we are not quite there. The American sports industry, for example, is perhaps the closest thing that we have to a true meritocracy. In most cases, an individual's bodily-kinesthetic intelligence will earn him or her a spot on the field or court of play. I use the term bodily-kinesthetic intelligence as opposed to athleticism, because I believe that many of the gifts and abilities that are displayed in sport are the result of intellect and go a step further than mere athleticism. *(I will explore this topic a bit further in a subsequent chapter.)* Still, there is much work to be done with regard to management and ownership for many organizations within the sports industry. For now, we will continue our discussion about America's history and how it affects the station many Americans find themselves in today. If we are going to make any long-term progress toward true meritocracy in this country, we must acknowledge a few things. The first would be what I believe to be one of the true foundational features of America: slavery.

The Foundation of a Nation

First, let us consider the Declaration of Independence, which immortally declares that "all men are created equal."[1] This bedrock document of American idealism was signed in 1776. Many of the men who penned and subsequently signed the document owned human property. The institution of slavery, however, which is well documented, began in 1619 on the shores of Jamestown, Virginia.[2] The two preceding facts beg us to ponder the following question: which year comes first, 1619 or 1776? The answer to this question may cause us to conclude that democracy and equality are NOT the foundations of America; rather, slavery is its foundation simply because it occurred first on the country's historical timeline. Similar to the construction of any building, the mechanism that is put in place first serves as the foundation upon which the structure is ultimately erected. Slavery was put in place long before the so-called ideologies of democracy, and thus, provided the means upon which America was built.

Not only did slavery show up in American consciousness nearly 160 years before democracy, many scholars credit slavery as the economic springboard that propelled America into becoming the wealthiest country the world has ever known. For instance, many historians and economists alike estimate the value of cotton, the primary crop managed by enslaved Africans, to be similar to the value of

16

Microsoft or Apple in today's economy.[3] In fact, Harvard University professor Sven Beckert positions slavery and cotton at the center of the world's economic boom. Beckert asserts that raw cotton accounted for more than half of the United States' exports during the first six decades of the 19th Century. The accumulated profits from those exports provided a lasting impact on the economy. Many cotton merchants, when they moved out of commodities, transitioned into banking and other sectors of the global market.[4]

Additionally, there are some industries that seem far removed from the cruelties of slavery but can be implicated just the same. The nation's earliest institutions of higher learning, including the Ivy League schools, accepted donations from slave merchants, allowed cotton manufacturers to sit on their trustee boards and educated many "Southern elites" who later returned to Southern plantations to provide leadership for business operations. Other Ivy League trained slave traders went on to be founders and administrators of some of the nation's earliest hospitals, libraries and religious institutions. Yale's first president, Rev. Thomas Crap, was a long-time slave owner. Jonathan Belcher, son of slave trader Andrew Belcher, became governor of Massachusetts after being educated at The Latin School in Boston and later Harvard College. Perhaps most disturbing, many of the nation's first medical schools used the corpses of enslaved Africans "for instructional dissections, wired their bones into skeletons for anatomical lectures, prepared their organs for display, even exhibited their skins and used them for decoration."[5] Beckert contends that "our world originates in the cotton factories, cotton ports, and cotton plantations of the 18th and 19th centuries; that slave plantations ... were in fact America's first big business."[6]

Cotton was not the only crop supporting America's financial strength and stability. Rice was another commodity that boosted the nation's wealth. Rice was the primary crop cultivated by enslaved Africans in the Carolinas and along Georgia's coast, making the region among the wealthiest of the thirteen original colonies. Rice was so valuable during the 1600s and 1700s that it was commonly referred to as "Carolina Gold." In fact, it was often acceptable for low-country South Carolinians to pay their taxes with rice. South Carolina, by that time, had led the nation in rice production for some two hundred years. The region was believed to be the top rice producing region in the world.[7] Yet, the economic value of the enslaved Africans was estimated to be the most significant. The worth of enslaved Africans was estimated at a value close to $10 trillion by today's measures, which represents approximately 60 percent of America's current Gross Domestic Product (GDP).[8]

At the time of the Civil War (1861-1865), the South's armed attempt at preserving its "Peculiar Institution," the price of an individual slave was at a premium and rising. An enslaved female was valued roughly at $1,000 and a male $1,500. Many were valued much higher if they were skilled laborers, such as carpenters, blacksmiths, boatmen ... etc.[9] Slavery was so valuable as a result of several converging factors, the first of which being the establishment of the Mason-Dixon Line. The Mason-Dixon Line, the border line formed between Pennsylvania and Maryland in the 1760s by surveyors Charles Mason and Jeremiah Dixon, essentially demarcated the boundary between the pro-slavery South and the anti-slavery North. Delaware represented the only pro-slavery state North and East of the line. Many scholars today continue to highlight the Mason-Dixon Line's significant correlation with the proliferation of slavery in the South.[10]

Another factor that contributed to the upsurge of slavery was the Northwest Ordinance. This seminal American document was established in 1787 by the Second Continental Congress to expand the country westward. Considered to be one of the most important injunctions in American history, it prohibited slavery North and West of the Ohio River. As a result, the Ohio River began to be observed in the same vein as the Bible's Jordan River, a symbol of freedom and fertility for many enslaved Africans. In the same year, the U.S. Constitution was formulated. It, too, helped to drive the value of slavery upward.

In fact, slavery was, by all intents and purposes, the impetus for the Civil War. Not only was it the impetus for the Civil War, it also instigated a significant amendment to the U.S. Constitution. The initial Constitution included language that all but condemned slavery, causing a few southern delegates to refuse their signature if the language was not removed. Thus, the Constitution was restructured as a result of the concession, prompting many scholars to later deem the document a pro-slavery manifesto. It is sometimes hard to fathom that these purportedly well-intended men conceded their morals in support of republicanism. Further, and perhaps better put, these extremely learned and high-minded men ignored probity for the sake of profit. In fact, of the five wealthiest U.S. Presidents in the history of this country, four of them lived in exorbitant luxury, on plush plantations serviced by large numbers of enslaved people, surrounded by ridiculous amounts of land, all because they refused to see Africans as people and chose to see them as property. It is important to note that two of these individuals are lauded as founding fathers, often universally celebrated, one as the brain and the other as the brawn behind the founding of America: Thomas Jefferson and George Washington, respectively.[11]

Lastly, the Oceanic Slave Trade Ban of 1808 significantly affected the value of slavery. This trade embargo made international slave trade illegal, thus preventing the importation of human property via the primary entry point for slave trade into the United States, the southeastern coastline. Ironically, with the passing of the Oceanic Slave Trade Ban, slavery in the southeastern portion of the country, in many regards, became inflated. This region of the country became the only territory on American soil where slavery remained a major economic stimulant.[12]

The converging of the aforementioned American regulations (The Mason-Dixon Line, The Northwest Ordinance, The U.S. Constitution and the Oceanic Slave Trade Ban), confined slavery to the Southeast, causing the value of enslaved Africans to spike. The catch here was that none of the four decrees outlawed interstate slave trade among Southern states. An enslaved African could be sold from Virginia down to South Carolina, Mississippi, Alabama or Florida at a premium, because at the time, the Southeastern United States was one of a few regions in the world where slavery was still actively being practiced. In fact, this phenomenon gave birth to the phrase "being sold down the river" in African American communities. The river in question, of course, was the Mississippi River. Again, the

Mason-Dixon Line, the Northwest Ordinance, the U.S. Constitution and the Oceanic Slave Trade Ban all inadvertently came together to underscore one of the cornerstone principles of basic economics: decreased supply coupled with increased demand or even unchanged demand typically drives price upward.[13]

A History of Degradation

As we continue to examine history's effects on modern Black life, we deepen our critique of slavery and assess, in detail, more of its consequences. Because of slavery's far-reaching economic implications, and in an effort to maintain its potency, many beliefs and attitudes were adopted in order to uphold slavery's influence and effectiveness. Unfortunately, many of these beliefs were anchored in cultural and ethnic racism that assumed the inferiority of African Americans based simply on the color of our skin. Although race is often used in attempts to differentiate between human beings, there are no significant biological differences among humans of different races. Race is almost always characterized by facial features, hair texture, or skin color. The underlying assumptions in these characterizations flaunt biology as the reason for the distinctions. These assumptions are gravely incorrect. However, and quite regrettably, many individuals have taken painstaking measures to prove the existence of race in biological terms, primarily in an attempt to prove the superiority of Europeans and their descendants against the inferiority of people of color.

Perhaps the originator of the movement to prove a biological basis for the concept of race was 18th century biologist Carl Von Linnaeus. Considered the father of anthropology as well as the father of the Taxonomy System, Linnaeus provided descriptions of the various characteristics that would become the delineation of the races. In one of his earliest publications, he described Europeans, a group with which he identified, as fair, acute, inventive, blue-eyed, gentle, and governed by laws. On the other hand, he described others in starkly different, often derogatory terms. For instance, he described Native Americans as copper-colored, content-free, obstinate, and regulated by customs; Asiatics as sooty, severe, haughty, avaricious, and ruled by opinions; and Africans as black, phlegmatic, cunning, lazy, lustful, careless, and governed by caprice. Linnaeus's descriptions, in addition to describing physical features, also implied personality traits. However, his depictions of the various personality differences were based solely on his opinion and lacked scientific evidence.[14]

Perhaps most disconcerting, he expressed his unfounded opinions in formal publications, prompting many to accept his rhetoric as truth. Regrettably, his erroneous opinions provided the foundation upon which a number of "scholars" based their pseudoscience. One such scholar was Johann Friedrich Blumenbach. If Linnaeus introduced the concept of race to the world, Blumenbach certainly championed its pervasiveness. An apostle of Linnaeus, Blumenbach attempted to classify and rank what he deemed the Five Principal Varieties of Mankind. The following excerpt from his doctoral dissertation, *On the Natural Variety of Mankind*, succinctly sums up his thinking:

Five principal varieties of mankind may be reckoned. As, however, even among these arbitrary kinds of divisions, one is said to be better and preferable to another; after a long and attentive consideration, all mankind, as far as it is at present known to us, seems to me as if it may best, according to natural truth, be divided into the five varieties; which may be designated and distinguished from each other by the names Caucasian [White], Mongolian [Asian], Ethiopian [African], American [Native American], and Malay [Pacific Islanders]. I have allotted the first place to the Caucasian, for the reasons given below, which make me, esteem it the primeval one.[15]

Here, Blumenbach attempts to make the group to which he belongs superior to all others. Again, his findings were not the result of scientific inquiry, but were based simply upon information received as a result of hearsay from traveling missionaries and tradesmen. Undoubtedly, a large majority of the tradesmen during that era were involved in the slave trade and thus relayed opinions about Africans that would further, as well as justify, their line of work.[16]

Slavery, indeed, existed long before the pseudo-science of Linnaeus, Blumenbach and the like; however, slavery most assuredly played a role, if not a major role, in how these "scholars" ultimately classified people of African descent. The abolition of slavery had begun to be a contentious point of debate during the era in which these men wrote, undeniably contributing to their ranking of Black people. Without a doubt, their classifications reflected common, though misguided, prejudices against people of color. Not only did they reflect widespread misconceptions about Black people, they were likely intended to reinforce and deepen those biases. Sadly, many of these misconceptions about Black people have seeped into the minds of countless individuals today. These perceptions are most detrimental when they rest within the minds of African Americans themselves.

The Presence of the Past

Post-traumatic slave syndrome (PTSS) is a term coined by acclaimed social scientist, scholar and author, Joy DeGruy. The theory takes into account the role history has played in creating the various negative perceptions, images and behaviors many African Americans have retained throughout the years. In particular, PTSS encompasses the adaptations that African Americans have employed over centuries in an effort to survive the repressive effects of chattel slavery. PTSS describes the transgenerational adaptations associated with the past traumas of slavery as well as the on-going effects of oppression. DeGruy believes that these past traumas have distorted the attitudes and belief systems of many African Americans. As a result, these beliefs and attitudes have developed into dysfunctional behaviors that often lead to less than desirable outcomes. DeGruy believes these dysfunctional behaviors have affected the lives of African Americans in virtually every area of our existence.[17]

Unquestionably, the experience of slavery was a consistently violent assault on the mind, body and spirit of the enslaved. Enslaved men, women and children endured grave and traumatic circumstances throughout the duration of their lives. And in an effort to cope with these unremitting attacks, the enslaved developed behaviors and comportments to ensure survival. Unfortunately, many of these practices, although necessary for survival at the time, were not advantageous to long-term well-being. And of further harm, many of these damaging beliefs and attitudes manifest themselves in the lives of African Americans today.

In her 2005 publication, *Post-Traumatic Slave Syndrome: America's Legacy of Enduring Injury and Healing*, DeGruy describes a scenario where a Black mother and White mother were engaged in a conversation about the academic and social progress of their sons, both of whom were classmates and teammates on one of their school's sports teams. The central theme of their brief conversation offered two very distinct viewpoints.

When the Black mother asked the White mother about her son's progress, the White mother described her son in glowing terms such as "talented," "gifted," "good athlete" and so on. However, when the White mother asked the Black mother about her son's progress, although very proud of her son, the Black mother talked about her son's sometimes less-than-fitting behaviors in school and at home, despite the fact that the African American student was outperforming the Caucasian student, both in the classroom and in the athletic arena. But, his mother neglected to publicly acknowledge his accomplishments, at least in this particular scenario.

Such incidences can be linked back to slavery. When a slave owner would notice and comment on the progress of an enslaved child, the enslaved mother or father would quickly retort with how awful the child was in an effort to protect him or her from being physically harmed or possibly sold to another slave owner. In those days, the enslaved mother's or father's denigrating remarks toward a child were done in an effort to dissuade harmful outcomes. Today, however, comments similar to those of the Black mother in the aforementioned scenario, though seemingly harmless, can serve to humiliate an African American child. Further, demeaning words similar to those above can permanently injure a child's esteem, as the child may be confused as to why his parent spoke so poorly of him. Unfortunately, in many cases, the child begins to internalize the scathing comments, causing grave effects to his self-esteem, especially when the painful comments are repetitive and have taken place over long periods of time.

In another example, DeGruy described a scenario where an African American mother was waiting to do business in a bank and had her small children with her. She kept the children so close they were literally wrapped around her legs. Anytime they attempted to leave her side, as small children often do in the exploratory stages of life, she quickly reprimanded and retrieved them back to her side. Meanwhile, a White mother, also waiting to conduct business in the bank with her children in tow, allowed her children to roam free. I believe scenarios like this contribute to an individual's internal locus of space, place and ownership. The Black mother was subliminally telling her children that the public space they were in was not theirs, while the Caucasian mother was sending the opposite message to her children. I experienced scenarios very similar to this as a boy. My mother would give my brother and I "the talk" before we ventured into a place of business. We were often sternly instructed to stay close to her side and to keep our hands off of any and all merchandise. I suspect this to be a similar situation for many children who grew up in African American households. Our parents were not intentionally marginalizing us; they were simply attempting to protect us from the gaze of those who would not see us merely as exploratory children.

Can you imagine the sense of powerlessness an enslaved parent experienced when a child was accused of an infraction by a slave owner? Imagine the terror a Black parent suffered when a marauding group of townsmen showed up on their front lawn, looking for a child accused of "eye-balling," theft, or worse. You must remember, many of our parents and grandparents actually lived through horrific moments not unlike the ones just described. So, for them to be hypersensitive toward the actions of their children in public places and spaces is quite understandable. My mother was simply attempting to shield my brother and me from the unwanted attention of those in real or perceived power. Though the gaze of those outside the African American community was often irrational and based on misguided stereotypes, it frequently rendered extremely harmful outcomes for those on the other end of that irrational gaze.

Unfortunately, such protections from parents today may prompt their children to believe that they do not own the world, but others do. My wife and I have made a conscious decision to allow our children to roam freely when in public places and spaces. In so doing, we indirectly suggest to our children that the world is indeed theirs and they are free to make of it what they will. It's a funny thing, though; I sometimes notice the perplexed stares of older African Americans when they see our children roaming free. I imagine they are looking on in bewilderment; I suspect they question, as well as disagree with our parenting strategies.

Widespread Myths and Misnomers

There are a number of behaviors that African Americans have adopted over the years that are less than ideal. Most were initially established as survival mechanisms. Others were never based on survival, but were created as a result of oppression. One such behavior has been our carte blanche acceptance of negative stereotypes and statistics about the African American community without any critical thought or thorough investigation. Many of these negative statistics and myths are long-standing misnomers that are, just now, beginning to be debunked. Take, for instance, the widespread myth that espouses the notion that there are more black males in prison than in college. This long-standing myth has recently been appropriately challenged by professor/researcher/scholar Ivory Toldson and filmmaker/community activist Janks Morton. These gentlemen appropriately and adequately support the fact that there are not more black men in prison than in college. In fact, according to Toldson and Morton, the document *Cellblocks or Classrooms?*, which originally espoused the now widely accepted theory, was attempting to admonish federal and state governments to provide equitable resources to advance social mobility and increase access to higher education instead of continuing to expand the prison industrial complex on the backs of nonviolent drug offenders. It was an attempt to highlight the nation's overuse of prison as a solution to social problems. Unfortunately, more than a few attention seeking journalists and pessimistic political pundits got wind of the critique and ran with it, but ran in the opposite direction of the authors' intentions.

To be clear, of the nearly 18 million African American males in the United States, irrespective of age, approximately 4.7 percent are in prison and 6.3 percent are in college. And if we were to narrow our focus to an age range of 18-24, the typical college age range, we would find only 164,400 in prison and 674,000 in college, a spread that represents a 4-to-1 ratio. Again, the authors of the habitually misquoted *Cellblocks or Classrooms?* were not trying to promote pessimism, but were attempting to encourage non-discriminatory economic, educational and criminal justice policies. Unfortunately, their words and intentions were taken out of context, and as a result, have been misconstrued for over a decade now.[18]

Black Fatherhood

Another misnomer about the African American community that has gotten traction over the years has been an acceptance of the notion that black fathers are absent. This is simply not true. Most of my friends who have children play a significant role in their children's lives. Even those who do not co-habitat with their children still maintain an active role in the lives of their children. I have never totally bought into the idea of the absent Black father. Most of the African American men I know are exceptional fathers. My own father, for example, who I often referred to as "the neighborhood's father," was and remains the consummate father. When my brother and I played Pop Warner football as kids, my dad was the father who would take the entire neighborhood of kids along with us. His car would be jammed-pack with neighborhood kids on our way to football practice. He would stay and help coach, though he was not an official coach. He would often get a coach's award at the end the season for being a volunteer coach.

He is also the father that many of us, to this day, go to for guidance; I refer to him as the Blue Collar Cliff Huxtable. Sans the humor, he always provides sound advice. He is the patriarch in the family who escorts my female relatives down the aisle, if and when their fathers are not around. As I have previously stated, he is the consummate father, not only to his biological children, but to others as well. Fortunately for many African American youngsters, they are often afforded the presence of father-figures like my father when their birth fathers are not around.

My brother-in-law is a great example of an individual who fathers in spite of having no biological children of his own. To date, he has fathered two children who are not his biological offspring. He has been and continues to be the only father my niece has ever truly known. He helped to raise her from the time she was around five years old and continues to be an integral part of her life now that she is an adult. He is also helping to raise a little boy that he and my sister-in-law have all but legally adopted. The young boy is the biological son of a family friend whom they have taken into their home. He spends a lot, if not most, of his time with my brother-in-law and sister-in-law. In many respects, my brother-in-law also serves as a father to the young boy's mother, who also resides with the family.

As indicated in a recent study, this has been the case for many Black families. *Fathers' Involvement With Their Children: United States*, 2006-2010 published by the Center for Disease Control (CDC) states that African American fathers, in fact, are more involved in their children's lives than fathers from other racial groups. Among many intriguing details, the report highlights the fact that many African American men parent children who are not biologically their own. From older brothers, uncles, stepfathers and grandfathers, African American children, many in spite of dire circumstances, receive love and guidance from caring men in their lives. The report confirms that, though many Black fathers live in separate homes from their children, they remain quite involved in the lives of their kids. A similar study by the Pew Research Center estimates that 67% of African American fathers who do not live with their children spend time with their kids at least once per month; when compared to only 59% of White fathers and 32% of Latino fathers in similar living arrangements, statistics like these appear to be ground-breaking, but in actuality, they have been pretty consistent for years.[19] But somehow it has almost been chic to make Black fatherhood synonymous with the term deadbeat. I find this to be quite insulting because, in many respects, I have defined my life by the fact that I am a full-time, hands-on, every day, loving father.

Black Achievement

Another false impression of the African American community has been the belief that some of us harbor an unyielding disdain for academic success and accuse high achieving peers of "acting white." This terminology got its birth as a result of a 1986 study conducted by academic researchers Signithia Fordham and John Uzo Ogbu entitled *Black Students' School Success: Coping with the "Burden*

31

of "*Acting White*.""Though the "acting white" phenomenon may have been a reality for Black students in the lone Washington, D.C. high school where the study was based, we should not generalize the phenomenon as something that all African American students experience.[20]

In recent years, Harvard professor Roland Fryer defined the term "acting white" as a set of social interactions in which students of color who regularly obtain above-average grades enjoy less social popularity than white students who obtain above-average grades. Fryer, as a result of analytical research, confirmed that "acting white" is a baffling reality in a subset of American schools. Quite interestingly though, his findings suggest that the way in which schools are structured correlated with incidences of the "acting white" phenomenon. Fryer's 2006 study, *"Acting White": A Social Price Paid by the Best and Brightest Minority Students*, found that the "acting white" phenomenon is unique to schools where African American students make up less than 80 percent of the total student population, with Black males faring the worst socially in such schools. Fryer postulated that African American male students were socially penalized seven times more harshly than African American female students in schools where Blacks made up less than 80 percent of the total population.[21]

Beverly Daniel Tatum's seminal 1997 publication, *Why are all the Black kids sitting together in the cafeteria?* may offer some insight into why this phenomenon occurs. She believes that the search for personal identity intensifies during adolescence, which includes racial and ethnic questioning for students of color. Students of color during this stage, when confronted with incidences that could be classified as racial assaults, gravitate to other students who may be experiencing similar encounters for support, thus forming a racially identifiable group. The group then may develop a system of beliefs and values that are in opposition to the school's dominant culture. When an individual within that group displays any attributes or characteristics of the school's dominant group, that individual is viewed as a traitor and subsequently treated as such.[22]

However, Tyson, Darity and Castellino's 2005 study, *It's Not a Black Thing*, found that the phenomenon exists for some black students, but is not as prevalent as once believed. They offer the position that, overall, social scientists have failed to empirically prove the phenomenon's existence, but suggest conversely that both high achieving White and Black students experience ridicule from low achieving peers in some schools in small measures. None of the middle school students of color included in their study expressed any concerns relative to their academic performance. Ultimately, they uphold that high achieving Black students across the sample were not, more than any other group, discouraged from enrolling in advance courses or doing well academically for fear of being accused of "acting white."[23] Interestingly, in schools where African Americans comprised more than 80 percent of the total student population, Fryer found no evidence that high academic achievement adversely affected students' popularity.[24]

My position regarding the phenomenon is this: generally speaking, there are very few students whose popularity is based solely on academic achievement. Popularity in school is based, most often, on one or a combination of the following attributes: good looks, fashion sense, humor, athleticism (bodily-kinesthetic intelligence), or an overall outgoing personality. To accept the notion that African American students harbor some sort of abstention from achievement is problematic. African Americans have always embraced achievement and always will. Because circumstances have been somewhat grave for many African Americans, the "acting white" phenomenon has to be examined from a variety of perspectives.

First, I believe that when the phenomenon occurs, students are not actually proclaiming that Caucasians have the market cornered on intelligence and are the only ones focused on achievement. I think that because African Americans are so communal and have largely depended on each other for survival throughout the years, perhaps when students notice a peer embracing and being embraced by an outside community, they come to the conclusion that their peer will soon leave the group. So, if and when African American students accuse a peer of "acting white," what they are really saying is, "It appears that you are positioning and posturing yourself to abandon me, and I don't want to be abandoned." In essence, the "acting white" phenomenon is more about abandonment than it is achievement. Besides, considering America's undying love for celebrity and entertainment, accusing African Americans as the sole purveyors of anti-intellectualism can be seen as yet another form of discrimination.

America's Culture of Anti-Intellectualism

Anti-intellectualism, in many regards, has become a significant part of American life. There are countless examples of the lack of value Americans place on intellectual or academic achievement. American heroes are typically entertainers and athletes, not scholars. America's pop culture has had a substantial impact on perceptions of intellect and educational achievement and could be placed at the center of recent dialogue regarding African American students and their so-called disdain for academic achievement. In a 2004 article titled *Acting White?: African American Students and Education*, Edward Rhymes references the advent of the terms nerd, geek, brainiac, and egghead and their relationship to academic achievement as foundational factors that contribute to the negative perceptions of African American student performance. Rhymes offered further that the ideology associated with the aforementioned terms did not originate in African American communities, but rather were the creation of mainstream America. As a result of the implications attached to those words, a desire to avoid the social death associated with those terms was established in American culture, resulting in academic achievement taking second place to social acceptance.[25] In comparison, if White high achievers do experience ostracism, they are labeled as nerds, geeks, brainiacs or eggheads, but this pales in comparison to Blacks being labeled as "acting white." These are social labels rather than racial ones and do not burden the White achiever with the impression that his or her achievement is racially inappropriate. On the other hand, the label "acting white' is a racial affront on the Black achiever and denotes that he or she is a race traitor.

Make no mistake about it; anti-intellectualism has long been one of the many characteristics of American society. Thus, it is my opinion that Americans in general, not just African American youth, have low regard for intellectual endeavor and/or academic achievement. I believe that the labeling of African American students as scornful of academic achievement is unfairly imparted.

Interestingly, there are multiple scholars who have offered the notion that African American students may have some legitimate reasons for associating academic achievement with Whiteness, if indeed they do. Historically, American public school curriculum has excluded the extended history, perspectives and accomplishments of African American people, thus causing a subconscious and sometimes conscious disconnect between academics and African American students. Coupled with the media's often pernicious depictions of African Americans, labeling them as scornful of achievement could be interpreted as a continued perpetuation of the vilification of the Black image.

Of further interest is another study conducted by John Uzo Ogbu and Herbert Simons. This 1998 study, entitled *Voluntary and Involuntary Minorities: A Cultural-Ecological Theory of School Performance with Some Implications for Education*, references the achievement levels of voluntary versus involuntary immigrants. Voluntary immigrants are defined as individuals who had chosen to migrate to a particular place with the hopes of forging a better life in their new environment. They typically expect better jobs, heightened political power and more religious freedoms. These minorities often embrace the customs of the dominant culture and view education as a pathway for success in their new environment. Involuntary immigrants, on the other hand, are defined as those who did not migrate to a place by choice, but usually migrated through enslavement, colonization or conquest. Most have been forced to be permanent parts of a society against their will. Most often, involuntary immigrants develop their identity in opposition to the dominant culture and as a result are often suspicious of societal institutions run by the dominant group, including schools, believing that the curriculum threatens and belittles their heritage.[26]

I believe this to be the impetus for the oppositional stance we notice in many young African American males. They often create a posture that, without analytical thought, would camouflage itself as simple rebellion. I believe, however, that this position is taken not merely as a form of rebellion, but actually serves as a form of protection. Time and again, African American males find themselves on the opposing end of a society that has convinced itself to view them with suspicion and fear. These views sometimes result in what feels like universal treatment, from others, as less than human. Some Black males, when they realize that others view them in this way, establish ways to withstand the onslaught. Often, these methods of protection (e.g. carrying illegal firearm or gang affiliation) are assumed against those that are nearest them, resulting in detrimental outcomes for African American males themselves, as well as their families.

For the past thirty years or longer, these detriments have been widely discussed and often fiercely debated by public officials, intellectuals and laypersons alike. The African American male's plummeting educational, social and economic status has been at the center of these conversations. Their disproportionate representation in America's penal and criminal justice system, their unemployment and under-employment rates, their homicide rates as perpetrators and victims and the fact that they are at the bottom of virtually every social statistic have many believing that they are simply inferior beings and incapable of doing well in life, leading to the suggestion that African American males are an endangered species. Though I recognize the Black male's plight, I disagree with the viewpoint that we are an endangered species. We have shown too much strength and fortitude to suggest extinction. African American males can achieve greatness. Many are doing so. Our dilemma demands a multitude of approaches that involve fresh and positive ways to address them. Chief among them is the way we see ourselves. Our beliefs about ourselves simply have to change.

CHAPTER TWO
AFRICAN AMERICAN MALES:
ARE WE AN ENDANGERED SPECIES?

*"We survived being described as mules, as having been put
on earth only for the convenience of white people. We
survived having nothing belonging to us, not your mother,
not your father, not your daughter, not your son.*
James Baldwin

*"You can only be destroyed by believing that you really are
what the white world calls a nigger."*
James Baldwin

We often hear people say that the Black man is an
endangered species. I clearly understand why such notions
are espoused. For starters, many Black males are receiving
an inferior education in schools where there is high principal turnover. In the districts where the majority of Black
male students attend school, their teachers will likely have

the least amount of classroom experience, with many of those same teachers lacking the proper certification and credentials.[1] Black males are suffering suspension and expulsion rates never before seen in the history of education in America. According to the 2008 *Schott Foundation 50 State Report on Public Education and Black Males*, African American young men have less than a 50 percent chance of graduating from high school in four years. And, when they graduate, there is no guarantee that they will attend college or acquire gainful employment immediately following high school completion.[2] There are also great possibilities that many will have considerable contact with the criminal justice system, if not be under its complete control. And, perhaps most disheartening, many in society will hold them solely responsible for all difficulties and limitations they face.[3]

It is clear that Black males are confronted with a number of obstacles that can serve as major setbacks or may even cause a complete derailment of their successful progression in society. It is, however, the opinion of many individuals that the issues Black males face should not be seen as solely their own, but should be seen as society's as a whole, especially since all of society is affected by the struggles of Black males regardless of socioeconomic background or ethnicity. According to Chris Crothers, author of the Foundation of the Mid-South's report entitled *Black Male: Why the Mid-South Cannot Afford to Ignore the Disparities Facing Its Black Men and Boys*, "The quality of life improves for all people when the social and economic issues that negatively affect those who are most vulnerable and/or disenfranchised are aggressively addressed."[4] Similarly, President Barack Obama, then Senator Obama, offered the following sentiment in the foreword of the National Urban League's 2007 publication, *The State of Black America - Portrait of the Black Male:*

> The crisis of the [B]lack male is our crisis whether we are [B]lack or [W]hite, male or female. The failure of our policies to recognize [B]lack men as husbands, fathers, sons and role models is being acknowledged, and we need a new ethic of compassion to break the cycle of educational failure, unemployment, absentee fatherhood, incarceration, and recidivism ... But it is too easy and sometimes too fashionable to demonize [B]lack men, especially young fathers, who have strayed. It's too easy to stereotype people even within our own community and to use them as an excuse for our problems. But in doing so, we degrade ourselves; we weaken the bonds of shared interest that are necessary to sustain us. We fail to give people the first chance they deserve and the second chance that we all sometimes require.[5]

In the same publication, the president of the National Urban League, Mark Morial, had the following to say about Black males:

> [E]mpowering Black males to reach their full potential is the most serious economic and civil rights challenge we face to today. Ensuring the future of the Black male is critical, not just

41

for African Americans, but for the prosperity, health and well-being of the entire American family.[6]

The reversal of the unpleasant position in which many Black males currently find themselves is an attainable goal. There are many strategies and circumstances that have proven ideal for Black men to succeed. African American young men who are academically successful are almost twice as likely to indicate feeling happy about the quality of their lives when compared to African American males with poor grades. This point speaks to the idea that being raised in a safe and healthy environment produces psychological stability, which then spawns well-adjusted and productive students. Ivory Toldson, in an influential Congressional Black Caucus sponsored document, *Breaking Barriers: Plotting the Path to Academic Success for School Age African American Males*, suggests that the academic success of African American males is more dependent upon their emotional well-being than that of their immediate counterparts, African American females.[7]

Another report, *Emancipatory Education vs. School-Based Prevention in African American Communities*, claims that Black males who simply aspire to attend college are more likely to perform better academically.[8] There are also links between nutrition and academic achievement, where students who consume raw fruits and vegetables on a regularly basis displaying higher levels of performance. However, perhaps most telling, African American males who have regular interactions with a male mentor or father-figure show considerable scholastic achievement. More specifically, Black males with their fathers in the home have higher academic outcomes. Of further interest, a father's educational level had a significant impact on a son's achievement level. And in general, parent involvement of both mother and father plays the most significant role in Black male scholastic achievement. Parents who are willing to regularly confer with teachers, who assist with homework, who encourage their children to do well by maintaining high standards and expectations in the home, typically produce high performing students.[9]

All of the preceding points attest that all students, including Black males, thrive when placed in the right environment. Not only do Black males succeed in the right environments, they also succeed as a result of proper expectations being placed upon them. We all are just as much products of expectation as we are products of environment. Unfortunately, the expectations that are placed on African American males often stem from widespread perceptions that they are incapable. Not only are there rampant perceptions of incapability, but these perceptions are coupled with severe contempt. This contempt comes from years of irrational propaganda that promotes a less than desirable image of the Black man, an image that transforms Black men into monsters.

Man or Monster?

The African American male's image has long been assaulted and battered by media, academia, Hollywood and much of American society. We have become acquainted with the all too familiar image of an African American male in handcuffs, arrested for an alleged crime, prompting many individuals to view Black males with suspicion and fear. The assassination of the African American male image began hundreds of years ago and will likely remain for many years to come. This phenomenon got its roots at the outset of the Trans-Atlantic Slave Trade, on the coast of West Africa and on many slave ships. In order to thwart insurrection, it was deemed necessary to emasculate the male captives.[10] The phenomenon continued during American chattel slavery, arguably the most brutal form of slavery known to mankind. In order to establish and maintain the potency of slavery, the African family as a whole had to be denigrated. With the male representing the head of the Black family, his persona— his very embodiment—had to be destroyed.

Immediately following Reconstruction and during the nadir of segregation and Jim Crow, the phenomenon reached arguably its zenith. Progressive African American males were often the target of mindless mobs, determined to put these "uppity niggers" in their places. Today, we continue to see explicit attempts to assassinate the Black male image. We specifically witnessed this reality with the release of Trayvon Martin's high school suspension record and toxicology information after he was murdered by self-appointed neighborhood watchman, George Zimmerman. We witnessed this phenomenon again when video images surfaced of what was believed to be Michael Brown shoplifting in a convenience store moments prior to being gunned down by Officer Darren Wilson of the Ferguson Police Department. The release of Trayvon's information and the alleged video images of Michael Brown were both attempts to insinuate some sort of justification for their murders. Noted scholar and author Earl Ofari Hutchinson, in his seminal book *The Assassination of the Black Male Image*, offered the following perspective about the Black male image:

> To maintain power and control, the plantation masters said that [B]lack men were savage and hypersexual. To strengthen racial control, late nineteen-and early-twentieth-century scientists and academics concocted pseudo-theories that said [B]lack men were criminal and mentally defective. To justify lynching and political domination, the politicians and business leaders of the era said that [B]lack men were rapist and brutes. To roll back civil rights and slash social programs, Reagan-Rush Limbaugh-Pat Buchanan-type conservatives say [B]lack men are derelict and lazy.[11]

Unfortunately, social status, wealth or political power do not exempt Black males from assaults on their image. We have seen this play out time and time again throughout history. We recently bore witness to this phenomenon as it unfolded with what seemed like around-the-clock analysis and re-analysis of professional football player Adrian Peterson's actions when disciplining his four-year-old son. Admittedly, Peterson's actions were a bit excessive and should have been addressed; I do not believe, however, that his faux pas should have resulted in any long-term suspension. The actions taken against Peterson were swift, with many calling for his permanent removal from professional competition. Meanwhile, non-Black men often trot away virtually unscathed after committing similar, if not worse, misconducts or crimes. For instance, U.S. District Court Judge Mark Fuller did not attract any immediate national media attention after brutally attacking his wife in an Atlanta hotel on August 9, 2014. In fact, nearly a month passed before his indiscretions were talked about on a national scale. The judge had been arrested but under what seems to have been a cloak of privacy and secrecy. It was even reported that the judge would check himself into some sort of treatment program that was "best for men in his situation and circumstances."[12] So, what is best for men in his situation and circumstances? It appears that what is best for men in his situation is very little intent to levy any serious claims against them, be it in the court of law or in the court of public opinion. There seems to have been no intentions to remove Mr. Fuller from his post as a federal judge, as he was scheduled to return to the bench just two days after the attack.

During the same time that Fuller's abuse was becoming broadly known, professional football player Ray Rice had been stripped of his contract to play professional football and took, rightfully so, a severe lashing in the court of public opinion for committing the same crime. In fact, as the two stories unfolded, it appeared that the judge engaged in much more sinister behavior by repeatedly striking his wife,[13] while Ray's incident consisted of, for all intents and purposes, a singular blow.

I am not trying to justify one man's actions and condemn the other's; both men were extremely iniquitous and at fault. However, it appears, as evidenced by the media's incessant coverage of one act versus its lack of coverage of the other, that there are subtle yet clear societal standards for Black men versus non-Black men. America continues to view the Black man as a brute, much as it has for hundreds of years, while elevating White men on pedestals, and, in most cases, exonerating them of any and all wrongdoing swiftly and under the cloak of silence.

Another related occurrence was the media's treatment of professional racecar driver Tony Stewart. Approximately one month prior to the media's firestorm around Mr. Rice's assault, Tony Stewart struck and killed another driver on a small dirt track in Canandaigua, N.Y.[14] While I acknowledge the media's initial coverage of the incident, much of the reporting suggested that it was merely an accident. The media, as well as the rest of the country, bought Stewart's claims that he never saw the other driver approaching his vehicle on foot before he struck him. In fact, about seven weeks after the incident actually took place, a grand jury decided that Mr. Stewart would not face charges for the on-track death of young Kevin Ward, Jr.

Stewart routinely drives around an oval shaped track at speeds up to 200 miles per hour, mere inches from his competitors. It seems that much of the media forgot the fact that Stewart is an expert driver. Not only is he an expert driver, he is considered one of the most proficient and best of the modern era, one who is known and even celebrated for his aggressive style of racing. Stewart, throughout his entire career, has habitually gotten into altercations with other drivers. Most of these exchanges have been Stewart's attempts to bully or intimidate fellow competitors. His rookie season in NASCAR was marked by a scuffle that took place with rival driver Kenny Irwin during a race in Martinsville, Virginia.[15] From then on, these kinds of incidences have practically defined his career. He has made a living out of being a tyrant on the track.

Stewart's ever-present temper is undeniable, which makes it somewhat reasonable to suggest some intentionality behind the incident that resulted in Kevin Ward, Jr.'s death. While I do not believe Stewart intended to kill Ward, I do believe he was attempting to intimidate him. Fortunately for Stewart, much of America believed him when he declared that his actions were unintentional. Only Stewart knows if that is, indeed, true.

Unfortunately for Black males, widespread acceptance has not been the outcome when we have proclaimed righteous intentions or even offered ourselves in surrender. Such was, disastrously, the case with regard to the now infamous and deadly encounter that took place between Michael Brown and Officer Darren Wilson in Ferguson, Missouri, on August 9, 2014. Most of the eyewitness accounts insisted that Brown was in a posture of surrender, with both hands raised when Officer Wilson unloaded twelve shots in his direction. Six shots struck Brown and ultimately killed the teenager. Brown's autopsy report by the Saint Louis County Medical Examiner indicated that the first four shots that entered his body, entered his right arm at an angle that would suggest his arms were in a raised position.[16]

World-renowned forensic pathologist Michael Baden, hired by Brown's family, would confirm the initial report's findings that the teen was likely in a position of surrender when the bullets riddled his body. Baden's investigation concluded that the first five shots that breached the unarmed teen's flesh were actually wounds that were treatable, injuries that Brown could have survived. The sixth and final shot that entered through the crown of his head was not treatable and became the fatal wound. And, according to three separate cause-of-death reports, the only way that a bullet could have entered his head at the angle in which it did, was if Brown were charging the officer face down, if he were in the process of falling or if he had already fallen, face first.[17] Again, according to all eyewitness accounts, Brown was not charging the officer, but was in a posture of surrender.[18] Another renowned forensic pathologist, Dr. Cyril Wecht, would substantiate Dr. Baden's analysis before and after a grand jury decided that Darren Wilson would not be indicted.[19]

After being fatally wounded, Brown's body lay in the street for 4 hours. He lay exposed for far longer than is customary or even appropriate. I believe his lifeless form being left uncovered for so long was deliberately done in an effort to send a message to Brown's peers and to his immediate community. Similar tactics have been used throughout history to intimidate and dissuade civil disobedience or disruption. Cunning slave merchants and owners used similar strategies to discourage the enslaved from running away or to deter group leaders from orchestrating revolts. Revolutionary and runaway slaves, when captured, were often flogged and sometimes executed in a public fashion to dissuade the remaining of the enslaved from following suit.[20] The Ferguson Police Department's (FPD) actions that day also harken back to a time when Black bodies where left hanging from trees like some sort of "strange fruit,"[21] left for others to witness.

Some may conclude that my supposition here leans toward hyperbole, but for what other reason would Brown's dead body lay in the street and for so long? I have come to the conclusion that his body was left there to subtly say to his peers, "This could be you, if you step out of your place." Much of the police department's actions that day and after substantiate my hypothesis. Not only were their actions brazen, they revealed a poorly concealed belief that Brown and people like him have no rights that should be honored. The Department of Justice (DOJ) Investigation of the FPD confirms this notion. The key findings of the investigation suggest that revenue, and not public safety, was the main focus of the department, causing unethical and discriminatory practices to take root in police operations. The following passage from the DOJ report perfectly captures the FPD's fundamental focus:

> Ferguson's law enforcement practices are shaped by the City's focus on revenue rather than by public safety needs. This emphasis on revenue has compromised the institutional character of Ferguson's police department, contributing to a pattern of unconstitutional policing, and has also shaped its municipal court, leading to procedures that raise due process concerns and inflict unnecessary harm on members of the Ferguson community. Further, Ferguson's police and municipal court practices both reflect and exacerbate existing racial bias, including racial stereotypes. Ferguson's own data establish clear racial disparities that adversely impact African Americans. The evidence shows that discriminatory intent is part of the reason for these disparities. Over time, Ferguson's police and municipal court practices have sown deep mistrust between parts of the community and the police department, undermining law enforcement le-

50

gitimacy among African Americans in particular.[22]

Armed with information like this, it would be safe
to say that the strained relationship between the African
American community and the FPD played a major role in
the confrontation that took place between Michael Brown
and Darren Wilson. A bigger tragedy, however, is the fact
that the larger community has accepted police practices and
procedures (i.e. traffic stops and arrest records) as evidence
of Black criminality. *(I will explore this thought a bit further
in a subsequent chapter).* This notion was made clear when
the larger community tacitly accepted the police department's position and neglected to collectively call for Officer
Wilson's identity to be released to the public. My hypothesis here is exacerbated by the fact that Officer Wilson was,
for all intents and purposes, placed on paid vacation while
the incident was investigated, and was later exonerated of
any wrongdoing. This point also highlights my argument
that White men are often shielded and protected from any
real consequences, even after they have committed serious
infractions. If and when the public begins to inquire about
what seems like lenient treatment, it is frequently stated that
"due process" is being permitted to run its course.

Conversely, it seems that when men of color engage
in similar or even lesser transgressions, corrective measures
are often swift, severe and uncompromising. We directly witnessed this phenomenon with both Adrian Peterson and Ray
Rice. The initial penalties levied against both gentlemen were
reasonable; they quickly changed, however, after considerable outcry from the community-at-large. I would classify

much of the outrage around these two gentlemen's actions as "selective outrage" because it appeared that the country's mania was extended toward these two individuals while simultaneously absolving others and sometimes themselves for similar infringements.

The country's collective indignation over Peterson's and Rice's wrongdoings harkened back to what seemed like ubiquitous resentment over National Football League star Michael Vick's mistakes a few years back. It seemed that every other person—political pundits, media personalities and laypersons alike—had strong convictions regarding Mr. Vick's role in the now infamous Bad Newz dog fighting kennel. I recall having several conversations with a number of individuals who were visibly enraged by Vick's behaviors. I vividly remember having these conversations, some over steak dinners and such. It always seemed strange to me that these individuals could be so upset over the death of certain animals while dining on other animals.

I realize that eating steak, chicken, fish and the like is not an illegal act, but the country's widespread outrage over Vick's actions seem to have taken a morally self-righteous and condescending tone. To me, it seemed that many had come to some sort of justification for their treatment of animals, while condemning Mr. Vick's treatment of animals. They had "selectively" decided what was inappropriate and off limits for the football star, while deciding the opposite for themselves.

[Note: Strangely, three of the aforementioned incidences (Judge Mark Fuller's Domestic Abuse, Tony Stewart's "Accident" and the slaying of Michael Brown) took place on August 9, 2014.]

Empowered Men of Color

*"Though the colored man is no longer subject to barter and sale, he is
surrounded by an adverse settlement which fetters all his movements.
In his downward course he meets with no resistance, but his course
upward is resented and resisted at every step of his progress. If he comes
in ignorance, rags and wretchedness he conforms to the popular belief
of his character, and in that character he is welcome; but if he shall come
as a gentleman, a scholar and a statesman, he is hailed as a contradiction
to the national faith concerning his race, and his coming is resented as
impudence. In one case he may provoke contempt and derision, but in
the other he is an affront to pride and provokes malice."*
Frederick Douglass, September 25, 1883

Sentiments that mirror Frederick Douglass's words above have been upheld for years in our society. Some individuals are practically commended for their idle activities, while others are condemned for their principled deeds. I have often wondered why such venomous and vitriolic positions were taken against National Basketball Association star LeBron James when he decided to leave the Cleveland Cavaliers and play for the Miami Heat in 2010. I distinctly remember that for virtually the first two seasons of James' tenure with Miami, he would be booed by any and all opposing team fans when he touched the ball. I clearly understand why Cleveland fans would have booed James, but what was the impetus for the entire league's hostility toward him?

James' decision to take fate into his own hands and leave Cleveland was no different from the business moves that team owners make in the name of the organization's bottom line. It is ubiquitously accepted when teams suddenly trade a player in the middle of the night in order to stay within salary cap limitations or to maneuver for choice draft picks. James was despised by virtually the entire country for making an intelligent business move. Even if his decision to leave Cleveland was the result of personal convictions, he was well within his rights to do so. But he was hated for it. Interestingly, he took a pay cut to join the Heat, a gesture that flies in the face of popular perceptions of professional athletes. Most are perceived as selfish and greedy individuals, who are capable of looking out for self only.

James' decision to leave Cleveland was broadcasted on national television and was dubbed, "The Decision." It was something never before done by an unrestricted free agent. The Decision was telecasted from a Boys and Girls Club in Greenwich, Connecticut, in an effort to raise money for the charity. The announcement, as a result of advertisement revenue, yielded $2.5 million for the Boys and Girls Club and raised an additional $3.5 million for other charities.[23] Again, this maneuver, organized by James, is antithetical to widespread perceptions of professional athletes.

James' move to Miami would prove successful. He stated that the impetus for his move was a desire to win, not just in the regular season, but to win championships. The Miami Heat did just that soon after James joined the team. In fact, of the four seasons he played with the Heat, the team went to the NBA Finals all four of those seasons and brought back two championships to the city of Miami. If someone were to offer me a fifty percent return on an investment, I would certainly invest. So, why were so many individuals upset with Mr. James' decision? Why were so many people spewing such venomous sentimentality in James' direction?

I believe that the vitriol stemmed from the fact that much of the country is not accustomed to seeing the deliberate and measured steps of a self-assured and empowered man of color. He was expected to be the $40 million slave that Bill Rhoden described in his extremely powerful book, *Forty Million Dollar Slaves: The Rise, Fall and Redemption of the Black Athlete.* In this pivotal publication, Rhoden describes African American athletes who have been conditioned to do things in a certain way and with certain individuals. He offers the metaphor that Black athletes are often shuffled along a conveyor belt of characters—agents, advisors, managers, financial planners, etc.—who control all aspects of their lives, with very little input from the athletes themselves.[24] But LeBron has largely been in control of his own affairs, which has made him into somewhat of a polarizing figure. His primary business partners are his childhood friends Maverick Carter, Rich Paul and Randy Mims, all young African American men. James' athletic achievements coupled with his business acumen sets him apart from the typical professional athlete.

James' friend Maverick Carter is the founder and CEO of LBMR, the marketing and management firm that orchestrates most of Lebron's publicity, marketing and promotional deals. Rich Paul played the power hand that recently moved LeBron back to Cleveland after his fabulous four year run with the Miami Heat. Paul was actually the partner who conducted most of the meetings with NBA representatives, including the phone call made to Cavaliers owner Dan Gilbert informing him of LeBron's return, while James enjoyed the rest and relaxation of a family vacation. Paul also represents other professional athletes, including LeBron's new Cavaliers teammate Tristan Thompson and Charlotte Bobcat Michael Kidd-Gilchrist. Mims is the third and final member of LBMR marketing firm, the company that has concentrated heavily on partnerships as opposed to deals where James serves merely as a celebrity pitch man. Their focus has largely been on shared ownership when deals are struck. Together, they are revolutionizing the sports industry.[25]

James has also been known to rub elbows with powerful businessmen outside of the sports arena. One such association has been his friendship with Berkshire Hathaway Chairman Warren Buffet. Buffet, currently the second richest man in the United States, occasionally offers business advice at James' request. The two, on the surface, would appear to be an odd pairing, but according to several sources, James and Buffet share several commonalities. Both are extremely driven and both have a keen eye for profitable business ventures.

James has also been known to fraternize with other business magnates, such as Dallas Cowboys owner Jerry Jones, Microsoft executive Steve Ballmer and music mogul Shawn "Jay-Z" Carter. He has clearly become antithetical to what has become, to some degree, the norm for professional athletes. These attributes make him an inadvertent target, because he and his business methodologies are largely in opposition to what is expected.[26]

Another uncompromising and polarizing African American figure has been boxing sensation Floyd Mayweather, Jr. Mayweather, too, garners quite a bit of public backlash for his unapologetic stance with regard to his boxing skills and business ventures. Mayweather is the recently retired pound-for-pound boxing champion, who has managed to amass a sizable fortune as a result of his 49 victories and 0 losses. Interestingly, Mayweather's fortune comes strictly from his work in the ring and does not include any endorsement deals, which is an astonishing feat, considering the boxer's $650 million net worth. This fact makes him independent of much input from outside influencers, making him one of very few African American public figures throughout history who has been in complete control of his own affairs. Mayweather and Mayweather Promotions CEO Leonard Ellerbe direct all business affairs for the boxing legend.

As a result of his undeniable talent and unblemished record, Mayweather often dictated the particulars of his fights, frequently to the chagrin of his opponents and their promoters. Until May of 2015, this had definitely been the case regarding the probability of fighting boxing great Manny Pacquiao. The boxing industry was virtually held in limbo as it attempted to forge a fight between the two stars. Many believed that Mayweather was afraid of Pacquiao and was avoiding him as a result. Others believed that Pacquiao had something to hide.[27]

Prior to 2015, when negotiations had taken place, Mayweather demanded that Pacquiao acquiesce to Olympic-style drug testing stipulations. Mayweather also insisted upon receiving the lion's share of the fight's purse. Pacquiao balked at the drug testing stipulations and demanded to split the purse 50/50. Mayweather consistently refused such arrangements raising the logic, of which I agree, that he was the undefeated champion and naturally should walk away with the largest share of the takings. And because of his impeccable ring history, unprecedented pay-per-view appeal and independent industry standing, Mayweather was able to determine his own fate and the fate of boxing's largest payday to date.

On May 2, 2015, the world finally got its wish and witnessed a Mayweather and Pacquaio fight. The match was the highest revenue-generating event in the history of the sport of boxing. The boxers agreed to a 60/40 profit split with contract terms that included strict drug testing performed by the U.S. Anti-Doping Agency. The drug screenings were performed before and after the bout and carried a four-year ban had either boxer failed the tests. With pre-and post-fight arrangements such as these, and because the event garnered $500+ million in revenue, many have deemed Mayweather boxing's brightest star ever. Though his status as boxing's brightest star is debatable, his keen business sense is less disputable.[28]

Like LeBron James, Mayweather too has a relationship with business tycoon Warren Buffet, a friendship that screams of Mayweather's thoughtfulness and intelligence. Luckily for these two gentlemen, their self-governing status, talent, intelligence and wealth buffer them from any significant hardships. Unfortunately, this has not been the case for all self-determining men of color throughout history.

Muhammad Ali, arguably the greatest boxer of all time, experienced great backlash because of his self-determining stance during a time when it was extremely dangerous to be so. Ali was exiled from boxing between March 1967 and October 1970, during what some believed would have been the peak of his career, when he was age 25 to 29. He was banished because of his stance against the Vietnam War. Ali refused to serve in the armed forces after being drafted, claiming that his Islamic faith disallowed him any engagement in violent acts. Ali's attempt at invoking his conscientious objector status was rejected by the United States gov-

ernment, resulting in him being stripped of his boxing ti-
tles, denied a license to box in all fifty states, sentenced to
five years in prison and fined $10,000 for draft evasion. His
refusal to participate in the war was interpreted by some as
high treason, but in actuality, he was simply taking a stance
against what he described as America's hypocrisy. He often
used the logic that "no Viet Cong ever called me a nigger," so
why should he cause them harm.

These circumstances not only caused Ali great suffering professionally, they also caused him great setbacks finan-
cially. He was forced to make a living by conducting speeches
and seminars on college campuses around the country. He
would eventually be allowed to fight again as a result of a
technicality observed by the Supreme Court during the ap-
peals process, but not before considerable damage had been
done to his career. Though he was a hero to many opponents
of the war, the layoff from the profession had affected his
boxing proficiency by many accounts.

Astoundingly, the Department of Justice was so un-
bending in their initial treatment of Ali, they even took away
his passport, restricting his ability to travel internationally.[29]
Interestingly, Ali was not the first African American public
figure whose passport was revoked as a result of systemic and
systematic controls. Paul Robeson also suffered a similar fate
during the early and mid-twentieth century.

Robeson, an acclaimed African American scholar,
athlete and activist, experienced public backlash and criti-
cism for his social and political views. A staunch advocate
for the liberation of African American and African people,
Robeson embraced many of the fundamental principles that
undergird socialism as well as communism. Robeson was a

steadfast opponent of racial injustice and spoke out against it frequently. He traveled abroad extensively to perform as a screen and stage actor, but also served as a voice for freedom. His political bravery and artistic prowess would be challenged and later cut-off completely during the McCarthyism era, a period wrought with Communist and Soviet paranoia.

He was blacklisted and boycotted by mainstream America, prohibited from performing on stage, screen, radio or television. His passport was revoked, disallowing him international travel for roughly a decade. By the time he regained the ability to travel abroad, the damage to his reputation had already calcified. As a result, he suffered from debilitating depression, survived a few suicide attempts and depended heavily on drugs in addition to being afflicted with other more conventional illnesses. He would eventually die from one of those illnesses, practically in abject poverty, having never received his just due for his many accomplishments or for his unwavering stance against McCarthyism and the like.[30]

Another African American thought-leader from the mid-twentieth century that sought a life of self-determination, but lived a somewhat lonely existence because of his political views and his sexuality, was James Baldwin. Baldwin, unlike the gentlemen referenced above, did not exactly encounter widespread backlash from governmental officials or from the general public. Before it could ever reach that point, Baldwin exiled himself to Paris, France. He described his departure from America as an attempt to avoid "the rage that many African Americans developed in response to [W]hite racism."[31] He had seen his stepfather wither away in complete bitterness, nearing insanity, under the overwhelming weight of racism and discrimination. Baldwin himself had contemplated suicide as a result of being denied service in a New Jersey restaurant once. He only contemplated suicide because he knew that any act of violence against his White perpetrators would result in the same outcome—his death. He did not want that for himself, so he left America in order to experience life as an unencumbered free person and writer. His move would do just that; from abroad, he gained a perspective of America that would inspire much of his most important and impactful work. His life in Paris provided him a perspective beyond the doctrines of Western imperialism.

Baldwin was one of the first scholars that would lay the groundwork for our thinking to stretch beyond a perception of America as a "melting pot," a viewpoint that insinuates an eventual disappearance of any distinctions among diverse groups. His new views embraced a national culture that included multiple voices and interpretations, one I would describe as a "salad bowl," a metaphor that emphasizes the importance of each distinct ingredient. His time on foreign soil would also provide him the opportunity to engage in real introspection that would lead to a true discovery of self and a full acceptance of his homosexuality. This discovery of self would also provide a clarity of thought and creativity that would spawn significant theories for the African American community's intellectual culture. In many respects, Baldwin's work prompted fresh ways to think about the African Diaspora. In fact, before Baldwin's writings, W.E.B. Dubois was perhaps the only African American thinker/writer directing the Black community to see itself as more than what the dominant culture had defined it as—slaves and former slaves.[32]

W.E.B. Dubois, a giant of a man, is considered the

father of Black intelligentsia. The first African American to receive a Doctor of Philosophy degree from Harvard University, Dubois was the epitome of self-determining Black empowerment. He spent his entire life fighting for equal treatment of African American people and all people of color. He strived to create a higher consciousness in African Americans.

Interestingly, he did not experience much racism or discrimination in his own life until he left Great Barrington, Massachusetts, for Nashville, Tennessee, to attend Fisk University. The South's treatment of African Americans, coupled with their responses to and their existence in this hostile environment, provided the foundation for his "dual consciousness" theory to emerge. This hypothesis would define much of his life and work.

The "twoness" of African American existence, as he called it, provided the springboard for his most pivotal projects. *The Philadelphia Negro*, a study he conducted that espoused the idea that a Black Elite called "The Talented Tenth" should lead the masses of Black folk, was anchored in his assumptions about the dualistic existence of African Americans. Though he later abandoned the "Talented Tenth" concept, his theory about the "twoness" of the Black mind was woven throughout most of his work that followed. Perhaps his most impactful contribution, *The Souls of Black Folk* became a cornerstone of Black thought as well as a pivotal component to the field of sociology. Dubois' work and leadership, in many regards, served as the impetus for the literary and artistic genius of the Harlem Renaissance movement. Many of the movement's writers and artists found inspiration in his work. Dubois also played a key role in the founding of the

National Association for the Advancement of Colored People (NAACP) and served as editor of the organization's monthly publication, *The Crisis,* for twenty years.

In the years leading up to the world's stock market crash, Dubois spent some time in the Soviet Union, resulting in his deeper appreciation for the foundational principles of communism. These views, of course, made him into a recipient of mainstream America's irrational gaze. His viewpoints were seen as militant and radical, which positioned him as an enemy of American idealisms. He would eventually be forced to retire from his post as chairman of the Sociology Department at Atlanta University and stripped of his passport, restricting his international peace and anti-war work.[33]

Near the end of his life, he moved to Ghana, West Africa, and helped to organize several Pan-African Congresses in an effort to free African colonies from European control. He died in Accra, Ghana, on August 27, 1963, a day before the March on Washington and Dr. Martin Luther King's famous "I Have A Dream" speech. In some ways, I believe the timing of his death was symbolic of his stance against the powers that be as well as an admonishment to the Black community. Though I believe he would have supported the coming together of so many people in the name of liberty, I believe he would have taken issue with the tone of Dr. King's speech. Because of his adamant stance against America, I imagine he would have wanted Dr. King's speech to be "I Have A Demand." I think "Dream" would have been too passive a word for him.

On the Brink of Extinction?

I began this chapter asking if Black males were an endangered species. I acknowledge the fact that life for the African American male in the United States has been arduous to say the least. I have, to my own discomfort, illustrated this point throughout the preceding paragraphs. It is true; African American males are forced to confront a society that, in many regards, is failing us. We are faced with various inequities that reveal themselves by way of our dismal representation in gifted education programs, but over-representation in special education and remedial programs. We are on the unfavorable end of unprecedented suspension and expulsion rates. We suffer from high unemployment and underemployment rates, resulting in bleak economic gains. As well, we experience disproportionate exposure to the criminal justice system. It is not particularly hard to unearth the tragic state of affairs Black males endure in large cities and small cities throughout the entire country. I believe these circumstances are a direct reflection of the long-standing and widespread stereotypical image of the Black man as a lazy, criminal-minded, ignorant, socially defiant burden to society. We must understand that these perceptions are rooted in misguided propaganda and are the product of low expectations.

African American males can and are achieving great successes in all aspects of our lives. Many of us view achievement as a natural expression of our very Blackness and use those achievements as vehicles to a better life for ourselves and our families. Our achievements are, most often, simply a matter of us being placed in the right environments and driven by high expectations.

Because of our many achievements and because the human spirit is so extremely resilient, I cannot agree with the notion that the Black man is an endangered species. Though I agree that there must be a concerted effort to improve our circumstances, we have endured far too much for far too long to suggest that we are on the brink of extinction. Furthermore, extinction implies that we are alone in our quest for survival. Most species that reach extinction are often isolated from other similar species, and are left to fend for themselves. Fortunately, we are not alone. We have many caring people surrounding us, mainly our women. This fact highlights, without a doubt, the most important reason why we are not in danger of extinction. In order to reach extinction, both sexes of a species must be in danger. I acknowledge that when the men in a community are affected, so too are the women, but our women have been too strong to be permanently derailed. Our women have willingly carried our community for decades.

Besides, human beings will not die without a fight; it is simply not in our nature. More specifically, African Americans will not die without a fight. We have fought not only to survive, but to thrive in this country. We have endured too many difficult days to even suggest an extinction of an essential portion of our community—our men. The African American community has rallied together to overcome many of the world's most arduous atrocities and yet, from these atrocities have come some of the world's greatest contributions. Many of these accomplishments exist because of our faith.

Let me explain what I mean when I say "our faith." I

am speaking of our spiritual faith, a deep-rooted belief in a Higher Power. I believe it was faith that sustained us through the horrors of the Middle Passage. It was faith that kept us strong in the cotton fields and rice paddies of slavery. It was our faith that saw us through the uneven fields of sharecropping and the absurdity of Jim Crow. It was faith that propelled us through one of our finest hours—the Civil Rights Movement. Equally, I am also talking about a faith, a deep belief that we have in each other.

When we examine the successes of the Black male athlete, for example, we find that many African American males have and will continue to excel in the sports industry, not simply because they are superior athletes, but because they have been surrounded by people who have a deep belief in their abilities to do so. Belief from others prompt these young men to believe in themselves. Accompanying this new found faith often is a steadfast work ethic. They work hard at their craft because they believe there will be fruitful outcomes.

In an earlier chapter, I insisted that we consider the abilities displayed on the field and court of play as more than mere athleticism. When we relegate these abilities to the realm of athleticism only, we tacitly agree to the notion that little to no work has gone into the finished results we see. Many of the talents that we see displayed in these brothers are God-given gifts, but I believe we are also witnessing a level of skill combined with those God-given gifts. The skill portion derives from the work they put into their craft. And, of course, the belief portion comes from a collective faith from them coupled with the community's faith.

Take basketball great Michael Jordan. His legend

originates with the fact that he was cut from his high school's basketball team as a 10th grader.[34] The fact that we now know him as arguably the greatest player to ever play professional basketball speaks to the fact that he worked to become better than he was as a high school sophomore. It also speaks of an internal as well as collective faith that propelled him to the stratosphere of the basketball world. His success derives from an amalgamation of a communal faith in him, his internal faith in himself and his intelligence.

Sometime ago, Harvard University scholar Howard Gardner proposed the Theory of Multiple Intelligences in his seminal book, *Frame of Mind: The Theory of Multiple Intelligences*. In this publication, Gardner identified eight ability areas that reveal themselves in the human brain: musical-rhythmic intelligence, visual-spatial intelligence, verbal-linguistic intelligence, logical-mathematical intelligence, interpersonal intelligence, intrapersonal intelligence, naturalistic intelligence and bodily-kinesthetic intelligence. He would later add a ninth, existential-moral intelligence. Gardner's theory argues that individuals learn in distinct yet identifiable ways with one of the intelligences taking a more dominant position. He offers further that the theory helps to disprove the prevailing view that asserts that everyone can learn the same materials in the same way and that learning can be assessed using universal measures.[35]

I believe that the abilities we witness in the sports industry go beyond mere athleticism and speaks more to aptitude or intelligence. What we are witnessing is bodily-kinesthetic intelligence. I am partial to the notion of intelligence because of its malleability. Intelligence is not a fixed phenomenon, but can be enhanced as a result of studying. Though athletes do not typically study in the way we have become accustomed to seeing it (i.e. books and computers), they spend a considerable amount of time analyzing and re-analyzing the body and its movements. We shortchange these scholars when we describe their accomplishments as ordinary athleticism. In so doing, we ignore the time, effort, faith and intelligence they have dedicated to their craft.

A few years ago, a young little league football prodigy from Malvern, Arkansas, was restricted from scoring touchdowns if he had already scored three touchdowns or if his team held more than a fourteen point lead. He simply had a knack for scoring touchdowns. The league that he played in instituted this rule in an effort to shield his opponents from embarrassment and to keep them enthusiastically engaged.[36] On the surface, these arrangements seem harmless as they attempted to protect the interests of players who may feel humiliated as a result of losing so severely. The arrangements seem to invoke a sense of gentlemanliness or sportsmanship. But, if we were to analyze these arrangements further, we may conclude that the young man's brilliance was being bridled.

In classroom settings, gifted and talented students are not restricted from displaying their intellect for the sake of others who may feel embarrassed. In fact, in many cases, gifted students are encouraged to assist others in an effort to make everyone better. Gifted students' intelligences are often used as tools to encourage and improve other students.

The limitations were, in effect, a disservice to the stand-out performer, his teammates and their opponents. The restraints placed on the young athlete did not give the opposing teams the opportunity to analyze their circumstances, make adjustments and ultimately improve as a result of those adjustments. The restrictions also prevented the stand-out and his team from improving upon their skills. We become better when we are given the opportunity to develop our skills and abilities further.

Bloom's Taxonomy, a framework used to understand the levels of learning, encourages a progression toward higher orders of cognition. It argues that true learning takes place when scholars are allowed to build upon things they already know or have previously applied in some way. Improvement occurs when individuals are allowed to analyze and evaluate a problem, situation or circumstance. Creation and innovation are what typically follows as students are allowed to devise new ways to approach a problem, situation or circumstance.[37]

I vividly remember an occasion, while in first-year College Algebra, I was lamenting an assignment because I thought it was remedial and addressed a concept I had mastered in high school. My best friend, Greg, who was also enrolled in the course, in his attempt to enlighten and encourage me, offered these words: "Rodney! Never be too smart to learn!" As much as I hated to admit it, he was absolutely correct. I now know that our professor had given the assignment to help us build upon what we already knew and apply it to what we were about to learn.

Restricting stand-out performers will not allow them to build upon what they already know. In fact, it may even effect the growth and development of those that surround them. This concept can be applied to the larger community as well. When we intentionally remove some of our community's greatest stand-outs, the entire community is stifled of growth.

Incarceration rates in America have increased exponentially in the past thirty years. These increased rates have largely taken place as a result of a so-called War on Drugs that has targeted Black and Brown bodies, male bodies in particular. Though seen as "criminals" and "derelicts" by much of society, in many cases these men represent the best and brightest in their communities. They are valuable assets to their children, their families and their communities. By removing these men from our communities, the entire country is ultimately stifled of growth.[38] The next chapter will explore this phenomenon in close detail.

CHAPTER THREE
MEASURING SUCCESS

"Even if you can't see something, that doesn't mean it isn't there"
Archer – Leader of the Gorgonites in the movie Small Soldiers

A few years ago, my good friend JC, after attending the funeral of the mother of one of his African American friends, asked me, "How does your family measure success?" Though I thought JC's question was interesting and thought-provoking, I knew there was an even more thought-provoking reason for his inquiry. During the funeral, one of his friend's siblings, when addressing the audience during the portion of the ceremony dedicated to friends and family to celebrate the legacy of the departed, shared his feelings of pride and admiration around the fact that neither he nor any of his siblings had ever spent time in jail. He was celebrating the fact that his mother had successfully raised him and his siblings as a single mother and had managed to guide all of them to college and not to prison.

My friend JC was perplexed by this particular measure of family success. He and his family had never, to his knowledge, viewed the avoidance of prison as a measure of achievement. In fact, he found it somewhat unbelievable that his friend's family saw it as a reason for celebration. What I have neglected to share with you to this point is the fact that my friend JC is of Euro-American descent. He comes from what may be considered a typical mainstream White American family and has had little to no experience dealing with America's criminal justice system. Unfortunately, this has not been the case for many families of color in America.

Our criminal justice system and those that are adversely affected by it are divided largely along racial lines. Most of the individuals currently under the control of the criminal justice system come from Black and Brown communities. And, it is projected that most of those who will come into contact with America's criminal justice system in the near future will come from Black and Brown communities—one of every three Black males born today can expect considerable contact with the criminal justice system, as can one in every six Latino males.[1] Without careful consideration, it would seem that people of color simply commit more crime in this country. If that were your assumption, you would be dreadfully mistaken.[2]

Because Whites make up 77.7 percent of the country's overall population, it makes mathematical sense that they would commit more crime statistically or at least constitute more arrests statistically, right? My hypothesis here is proven correct based upon Federal Bureau of Investigation (FBI) records. According to the FBI's 2012 arrest records, Whites accounted for 6.5 million of the 9.3 million total recorded arrests, a number that constitutes 69.3 percent of all arrests. Meanwhile, African Americans accounted for 2.6 million arrests, a number that represents 28.1 percent of all arrests. When we consider proportionality, however, African Americans make up roughly 14 percent of the country's overall population, but accounted for 28.1 percent of all arrests in 2012.[3] It is mind-boggling to think through this reality; African Americans were arrested at a rate that doubles our overall portion of the population. In the state where I live, African Americans make up roughly 10.9 percent of the state's population and accounted for 17.3 percent of the traffic stops made by police officers in 2013. And of those stops, Blacks were arrested 7.7 percent of the time.

These numbers do not seem very alarming until they are compared with the statistics that are associated with White Americans in my state. Whites make up 82.7 percent of the state's population and accounted for 79.2 percent of stops in 2013, but interestingly only constituted 4.2 percent of the arrests. Of further interest, Whites were found with contraband 26.3 percent of the time and Africans Americans 18.8 percent of the time. Since Whites were found holding contraband at a higher percentage rate than African Americans, why were they arrested at a rate lower than African Americans?

When looking at Latino and Native American stop, search and arrest rates in my state, the numbers are somewhat similar to African Americans but do not draw considerable alarm when examining their disparity indices. All ethnicities with the exception of African Americans reflect a disparity index that is less than a value of 1, according to 2013 statistics. A disparity index that exceeds the value of 1 indicates that a group's proportion of traffic stops surpasses its portion of the population. The African American disparity index was 1.59, which signifies an over-representation in stops. All other groups came in at values less than 1: Whites (.96); Latinos (.61); Asians (.52); Native Americans (.25) and others (.53).[4]

Again, on the surface, statistics like these may cause one to assume that African Americans are simply more likely to commit crimes. Trust me, there are scores of individuals who believe people of color, mainly African Americans, are more prone to engage in criminal activity. A 2004 study entitled *Black Criminal Stereotypes and Racial Profiling* substantiates this point. The report revealed that 54 percent of Whites that participated in a General Social Survey believed that Blacks are more prone to violence. The analysis also uncovered a widespread belief that characterized Blacks, more than any other racial group, as violent, more likely to abuse drugs and more likely to engage in crime.[5] Another nationwide report in the same year, *Racial Typification of Crime and Support for Punitive Measures,* showed that the general public believed that Blacks were involved in a greater percentage of violent crimes than statistics actually substantiated.[6]

Interestingly, our neighbors to the north revealed a similar perception of Black Canadians as indicated in a 1996 study called *Perceptions of Race and Crime in Ontario.* The study showed that 65 percent of a random sampling of Canadians believed that Black people committed more crime than other racial and ethnic groups.[7] In America, three years prior to the Canadian study, a 1993 Anti-Defamation League survey corroborate the aforementioned opinions. It revealed that 60 percent of White Americans polled believed at least one harmful stereotype about African Americans. These harmful beliefs were in regard to perceived aggressiveness, violence, work ethic and welfare assistance.[8] And perhaps the most threatening findings come from tests that assess implicit associations. Repeatedly, these tests reveal subconscious associations between Black faces and terms such as criminal, evil, failure and vile. These tests showed that many individuals exhibit difficulty linking Black faces to positive attributes or pleasant words. And, perhaps most disturbing of all, these tests exposed the country's deep-rooted fear of African Americans, Black males in particular. In nationwide, statistically significant Implicit Association Tests that measure racial views, 70 to 87 percent of Caucasians showed biased attitudes toward African Americans. In fact, on many occasions, the area of their brains that responds to danger, the amygdalae, activated when African American faces were flashed on a computer screen for a mere fraction of a second.[9]

In light of these findings, it would be safe to suggest that implicit bias may have led to the warped nationwide arrests rates mentioned earlier. These rates speak more to the country's inherent prejudices than they do to the criminality of Africans Americans and other people of color. Unfortunately, these biases have been such a covert aspect of American life for so long that it is extremely challenging to prove their existence. I believe these obscurities are linked to our understanding, or lack thereof, of America's deep-seated culture of power.

Culture of Power

   If you are a person of color in America, an individual who practices any religion other than Christianity, a woman or even a child, then you understand culture of power. Noted author and activist, Paul Kivel, succinctly describes this phenomenon in *Culture of Power,* an essay that is part of a diversity anthology entitled *What Makes Racial Diversity Work in Higher Education:*

> If you are a woman who has ever walked into a men's meeting, or a person of color who has walked into a white organization or a child who has walked in the principal's office, or a Jew or Muslim who has entered a Christian space then you know what it is like to walk into a culture of power that is not your own. You may feel insecure, unsafe, disrespected, unseen or marginalized. You know you have to tread carefully.

> Whenever one group of people accumulates more power than another group, the more powerful group creates an environment that places it members at the cultural center and other groups at the margins. People in the more powerful group (the "in" group) are accepted as the norm, so if you are in that group it can be very hard for you to see the benefits you receive.

> Because I'm male and live in a culture in which men have more social, politi-

cal, and economic power than women, I often don't notice that women are treated differently than I am. I'm inside a male culture of power. I expect to be treated with respect, to be listened to, and to have my opinion valued. I expect to be welcomed. I expected to see people like me in positions of authority. I expect to find books and newspapers that are written by people like me that reflect my perspective, and that show me in central roles. I don't necessarily notice that the women around me are treated less respectfully, ignored, or silenced; that they are not visible in positions of authority nor welcomed in certain spaces; that they pay more for a variety of goods and services; and that they are not always safe in situations where I feel perfectly comfortable.

Remember when you were a young person entering a space that reflected an adult culture of power – a classroom, store, or office where adults were in charge? What let you know that you were on adult turf and that adults were at the center of power? ... They made the decisions. They might have been considerate enough to ask me what I thought, but they did not have to take my concerns into account. I could be dismissed at any time, so I learned to be cautious ... I felt I was under scrutiny. I had to change my behavior—how I dressed ("pull up your pants", tuck in your shirt"), how I spoke ("speak up", "don't mumble your words"), even my posture ("sit up", "don't slouch", "look me in the eye when I'm talking to you")—so that I would be accepted and heard. I could not be as smart as I really was or I'd be considered a smart aleck. I had to learn adults' codes, talk about what they wanted to talk about, and find allies among them—adults who would speak up for my needs in my absence. Sometimes I had to cover up my family background and religion in order to be less at risk from adult disapproval. And if there were any disagreement or problem between an adult and myself, I had little credibility. The adult's word was almost always believed over mine.

The effects on young people of an adult culture of power are similar to the effects on people of color of a white culture of power ...[10]

This notion of an existing culture of power has been challenging to assert in a society that believes it is structured on the principles of hard work, fairness and equal opportunity. We Americans rest on a ubiquitous belief that hard work always leads to success. While I can agree with the country's commitment to hard work, I cannot agree that hard work always results in successful outcomes. Who worked harder than enslaved Africans, or Black sharecroppers, or Black Pullman porters or Black domestics? Again, I can agree with the universality of potential in America; I cannot, however, agree in the ubiquity of opportunity. Opportunities that result in success have come slow for certain sectors of our society, while it has been the exact opposite for other sectors. If we can agree that there are populations in our society that are under-served, we must also agree that there are populations that have been over-served.

Again, attempts to confirm the existence of this culture of power have been extremely difficult to affirm, mainly because of its links to the extremely elusive concept of Whiteness. Not only does this culture exist, it dictates how those who are a part of the culture judge and view those who are outside the culture. America's culture of power is synonymous with a culture of Whiteness. This pervasive, yet obscure, identity standard is woven into and throughout the fabric of America's overarching ethos. It is widely accepted but rarely spoken or acknowledged. It has been an unexpressed phenomenon, largely because an acknowledgment of this concept inadvertently carries with it recognition of the existence of White privilege. Any such acceptance comes with an acknowledgement of racism and its ubiquity.[11]

There is no denying the role that race and racism have played throughout American history. Beverly Daniel Tatum compares racism to living in a city affected by smog, offering the analogy that racism, like smog, sometimes is so thick it is visible and other times it is less apparent, but always present causing individuals to breath it in, whether they want to or not.[12] Tim Wise says that, "Race may be a scientific fiction, but is a social fact; one that none of us can escape no matter how much or how little we talk about it."[13] Perhaps a larger problem with this phenomenon known as racism is the way it has been conceptualized throughout American history. Michelle Alexander, in what I believe to be one of the most powerful books of the 21st century, *The New Jim Crow*, described our collective view of racism as follows:

> As a society, our collective understanding of racism has been powerfully influenced by the shocking images of the Jim Crow era and the struggle for civil rights. When we think of racism we think of Governor Wallace of Alabama blocking the schoolhouse door; we think of water hoses, lynchings, racial epithets, and "[W]hites only" signs. These images make is easy to forget that many wonderful, good-hearted [W]hite people who were generous to others, respectful of their neighbors, and even kind to their [B]lack maids, gardeners, shoe shiners—and wished them well—nevertheless went to the polls and voted for racial segregation, actually believing they were doing [B]lacks a favor or believing the time was not "right" for equality. The disturbing images from the Jim Crow era also make it easy to forget that many African Americans were complicit in the Jim Crow system, profiting from it directly or indirectly or keeping their objections quiet out of fear of the repercussions. Our understanding of racism is therefore shaped by the most extreme expressions of individual bigotry, not by the way in which it functions naturally, almost invisibly (and sometimes with genuinely benign intent), when it is embedded in the structure of a social system.

The unfortunate reality we must face is that racism manifests itself not only in individual attitudes and stereotypes, but also in the basic structure of society.[14]

Peter Heinze, in a 2008 article, *Let's Talk About Race, Baby*, supports the above notions and supposes further that the Euro-American worldview, America's prevailing viewpoint, tilts heavily toward dichotomous ways of thinking, and as a result, has influenced the widespread misconception that the United States is comprised of two groups of people, those who are racist and those who are not racist. While this dualistic way of thinking, in some respects, is a function of the way the human brain is wired, it contributes to a number of societal misconceptions. This way of thinking has led to the erroneous belief that America is now a colorblind society and contributes to the tendency for most individuals to perceive themselves as non-racist. Also, along these same lines comes the widespread propensity to restrict the label of "racist" only to the known hatemongers in our society, White supremacists, the Klu Klux Klan, Neo-Nazis, Skinheads and other hate crime perpetrators.[15]

I suspect that this type of thinking, in some ways, allow individuals to explore the hidden aspects of their own racist ways of thinking, but under the cloak of privacy. This way of thinking allows the masses to privately examine characteristics and traits about themselves that they would prefer not to acknowledge. This, I believe, is classic scapegoating, where all that is bad is projected onto certain groups, "the bad apples," relieving the rest of society from any real introspection or critical reflection. Having a group or groups that we can point to as the known culprits in society lets the rest of the country off the hook. The majority of Americans would rather exempt themselves from acknowledging the more common, subtle forms of racism that create the unearned and unequal privilege that has led to widespread advantages for some and disadvantages for others.

Racism should not be seen as a linear concept with an "either/or" attribute, but rather be seen as a much more fluid phenomenon that happens along a continuum. Individuals fluctuate back and forth between confusion, denial, acceptance and growth along this continuum. Many scholars believe that simply because we reside in America, we cannot avoid mythical images of White superiority coupled with concurrent stereotypical images of the inferiority of people of color. And because of these images, a subconscious, tacit form of racism takes root, causing some Whites to view only the "others" as having a race, which renders them "abnormal," while simultaneously viewing themselves as "unraced and normal." Often, when the topic of race, diversity or culture is presented, it is often assumed to be in reference to persons of color only, which is inherently racist. Not racist in the dichotomous way we have grown to know it, but racist in the assumption that Whites are raceless, and in an interpretation of culture or cultural engagement as an opportunity for Whites to enlighten, assist, parent or patronize the "others" in our society.[16]

I believe that individuals cannot simply proclaim that they do not have racist thoughts. I suspect that even individuals who actively engage in anti-racism activism, those who have engaged in extensive self-reflection regarding their own racism, harbor racist thoughts, whether consciously or subconsciously. This point causes me to recall a scenario that noted scholar and anti-racism activist Tim Wise described in perhaps his most impactful composition, *White Like Me.* Wise referenced an occasion when he stepped onto an airplane for one of his many trips to speak out against race and racism. As he entered the aircraft, he happened to glance into the cockpit and noticed two African American pilots. He immediately felt concern for the safety of the flight. After he reached his seat he began to examine his thoughts and concluded that he, perhaps, was on the safest plane in America. He came to this conclusion because he rationalized that the African American pilots had probably gone through far more scrutiny than the average White pilot because of widespread beliefs in Black inferiority. He suspected that these gentlemen were more than qualified to fly the aircraft because they had likely proven their competency over and over again as a result of these stereotypical views. Wise traveled to his destination with the assurance of those final thoughts; that these gentlemen were more than qualified to fly the aircraft.[17]

Here we have one of the foremost anti-racism voices in the country wrestling with deep-seated thoughts of racism. If this kind of thinking occurs in the mind of an individual who has consciously and actively engaged in countering the effects of racism, then surely this way of thinking seeps into the minds of everyday individuals navigating the sways of American life. A much more disturbing form of the phenomenon, however, occurs among people of color themselves. I believe this to be the case in the deadly confrontation that took place between George Zimmerman and Trayvon Martin.

Zimmerman, a person of Latin American descent,

bought into the widespread belief of the criminality of young black males. This point was proven when we audibly heard Zimmerman mumble, "They always get away," on the recorded 911 call. Many of us know that he was referring to young African American males specifically. Zimmerman is no different from many, if not most, Americans. He has not been exempted from the bombardment of media images that have repeatedly portrayed young African American males as criminal-minded derelicts. I am well aware that many of us suffer from "Others-are-biased-but-I'm-not-biased" Syndrome, but if we are honest with ourselves, we would take ownership of our many biases. Ownership of these biases, I believe, is the first step toward healing from them. But, because we have not, racism, discrimination and marginalization all maintain a significant level of potency in our society.

Even I, an African American male who understands the effects of these images, fall prey to them from time to time. I remember one evening, while living in Nashville, Tennessee, my wife and I were leaving a restaurant after enjoying an evening meal. As we were approaching our vehicle, I noticed a young African American male dressed in a hoodie approaching from the opposite direction. I immediately placed my keys through my knuckles in an effort to protect my wife and me in case a confrontation ensued. As we got closer, the young man looked up and greeted us, "Good Evening Ma'am and Sir, this is some unusually cold weather we're having, huh?" I immediately felt an internal embarrassment. I assumed that he was wearing a hoodie to conceal his identity in an effort to accost us, when he was merely shielding himself from the unusually cold weather we were experiencing in the region. I am sure that many of you have had similar experiences. We automatically assume that young Black males are criminals and will cause us harm in some way. We are not totally at fault for arriving at these conclusions. We have been subjected, for many years, to images of the Black man as a criminal-minded brute. These images have led to a prison system that is made up, largely, of Black and Brown men.

The Color of Crime

The criminal image of the Black male is certainly not new, but it definitely has grown exponentially in recent years as a result of America's so-called War against Crime, and more specifically, its ostensible War on Drugs. This war was launched in a widespread way in the early 1970s under President Richard Nixon's administration. It was later diminished in some ways during the late 1970s under President Jimmy Carter's administration. Carter, in fact, used the decriminalization of marijuana as part of the campaign platform that ultimately landed him in the White House. The War, however, regained its steam under President Ronald Reagan's administration in the 1980s. It actually skyrocketed under Reagan's administration as a result of the "Just Say No" campaign led by his wife, Nancy.

Interestingly, the War on Drugs is not altogether a new phenomenon. It had its first go-around in the 1870s when anti-opium laws were erected, specifically against Chinese immigrants. The first anti-marijuana laws were directed at Mexican Americans and Mexican immigrants in the 1910s and 1920s. And the first anti-cocaine laws were aimed at Black men in the South during the early 1900s. These early anti-drug restrictions seem to have been directed at certain populations of people as opposed to being based on any scientifically proven risks associated with the drugs or any rampant overuse by the aforementioned communities.[18]

It has always seemed strange to me that some drugs are perfectly legal while others are deemed illegal. We are bombarded with prescription drug commercials aimed at a number of conditions and ailments, from high cholesterol to erectile dysfunction. Without sounding like a conspiracy theorist, it seems that there are economic implications to this war on drugs, considering that we are driven toward certain drugs but led to prison for our contact with others.

Look, I am not making a case for the legalization of any drug with my supposition here. In fact, with the exception of smoking a little marijuana during my college years, I have never been a regular drug user, definitely not an abuser. I have not even had an alcoholic drink in over ten years, so my comments are not a backdoor attempt to justify my vices. I am simply making what I hope would be seen as an astute observation.

It has also emerged over the years that certain individuals are penalized differently for similar, if not the same, kinds of drug infractions. I imagine it is safe to say that most Americans would find it hard to believe that illicit drug use and distribution are remarkably similar across ethnicities. As Michelle Alexander highlights in *The New Jim Crow*:

> People of all races use and sell illegal drugs at remarkably similar rates. If there are significant differences in the surveys to be found, they frequently suggest that [W]hites, particularly

86

[W]hite youth, are more likely to engage in illegal drug dealing than people of color. One study, for example, published in 2000 by the National Institute on Drug Abuse reported that [W]hite students use cocaine at seven times the rate of [B]lack students, use crack cocaine at eight times the rate of [B]lack students, and use heroin at seven time the rate of [B]lack students. That same survey revealed that nearly identical percentages of [W]hite and [B]lack high school seniors use marijuana. The National Household Survey on Drug Abuse reported in 2000 that [W]hite youth aged 12-17 are more than a third more likely to have sold illegal drugs than African American youth. Thus the very same year Human Rights Watch was reporting that African Americans were being arrested and imprisoned at unprecedented rates, government data revealed that [B]lacks were no more likely to be guilty of drug crimes than [W]hites and that [W]hite youth were actually the most likely of any racial or ethnic group to be guilty of illegal drug possession and sales... [W]hite youth have about three times the number of drug-related emergency room visits as their African American counterparts.

Yet, the reverberating image of a drug dealing criminal is the face of an African American male. And, similar to the methodologies of slavery, in order to sustain the image of the *criminalblackman*,[19]

Black males have to be labeled as criminals across the board and must be given this label early in life.

Officially, there is no universal rites of passage into manhood for Black males. Sure, there are several impactful youth development programs and organizations that are doing great work to help Black boys develop into productive men. But unfortunately, these organizations and programs are not reaching as many young men as planned. Regrettably, contact with the criminal justice system has served as a twisted rites of passage program for many young Black men. Sadly, this rites of passage program has even been embraced by a small percentage of Black males. Some have instituted a system of "street cred" as a result of their contact with the system. For others, in addition to serving as a demented rites of passage mechanism, contact with the criminal justice system serves as their identity awakening. Many discover that they are indeed "Black" as a result of their first encounter with law enforcement.

William E. Cross described the identity development for some African Americans as the discovery of Nigrescence. He believes that this process happens in five stages: Pre-encounter, Encounter, Immersion, Emersion, and Internalization. The Pre-encounter stage describes a person's identity before he or she encounters a situation that makes them aware of their Blackness. This stage may include the understanding that a dominant culture exists, but nothing has taken place to cause dissonance with the dominant group. The Encounter stage, as alluded to above, happens when an individual is forced to grapple with not only their Black identity as it relates to the world around them, but their social status as compared to other ethnicities in society. Often, this stage involves a confrontation with race or its evil offspring, racism. The Immersion stage commonly ushers in complete absorption of a new found Blackness. Individuals in this stage may, as they fully embrace their own identity and ethnicity, distance themselves from other ethnicities. The Emersion stage goes hand-and-hand with the Immersion stage and often includes a quest to align oneself with others who are experiencing a similar journey. In the final stage, Internalization, individuals typically learn to embrace their identity within a healthy context. A life-long commitment to one's own community is understood during this stage, while still maintaining the ability to forge relationships with people from other racial and ethnic groups.[20]

Encounters with the criminal justice system often thrust young Black men into permanent awareness of their identity. Not only are African American men aware of this threat, but others are consciously aware of this looming danger as well. A few years back, a former student of mine shared with me the encounter that caused him to become intimately aware of his identity as a Black man. Though he had become cognizant of his identity earlier in life, this new encounter served as a glaring reminder.

My student had been walking to campus from his off-campus apartment when two Caucasian female friends stopped and offered him a ride to campus. After joining them in the vehicle, they all begin to take part in smoking a "joint" together. As a result, the young ladies, more than he, had become inebriated to the point that neither could drive. Because he was in better condition to drive, he offered to chauffeur them to campus. When he took the driver's seat, the young lady who owned the vehicle flippantly said to him,

"Don't wreck my car, because if you do, I will tell the cops that you kidnapped us and was trying to steal my car." Though, deep down, he believed she was joking, he realized at that moment that not only was he aware of his Blackness, his female friend was fully aware of his identity as well. He recanted his offer to drive and decided to walk to campus with his newly reconfirmed identity.

Though this scenario did not exactly involve an encounter with the criminal justice system, it certainly was the looming antagonist of the scenario. The young lady revealed that she was well-aware of the *criminalblackman* image and shared her awareness with my student. I did not share this story as an attempt to minimalize recreational drug use or to claim that my student's female friend is a hatemonger. To the contrary, I believe she sincerely considered him a friend, but that fact does not negate the reality that she has been significantly influenced by the resonating image of the *criminalblackman*. We all have been influenced by this persistent image.

Simply because you believe that you are not biased against Africans Americans does not mean that your beliefs actually coincide with your true feelings. As illustrated in an earlier part of this chapter, many of us harbor implicit biases toward African Americans as revealed through Implicit Association Tests. Amazingly, a number of the tests' participants were African Americans, who we would assume harbored no biases against themselves.

An understanding of the racialized history that our racialized thoughts and beliefs are based upon will help us to unpack both our conscious and unconscious biases. We have created images that, in the end, distort our judgments and

and decisions with regard to what is fair and just. In many respects, it has created a sense of apathy on both sides of the track, in Black communities as well as in communities of power. On one side, mainstream America has canvassed society, campaigning the message that young + Black + male = criminal. In Black communities, many of us have tacitly accepted and even complacently normalized the Black male image as criminal. Some individuals have concluded that it is a matter of pathology, that Black males are simply born with the propensity to commit crime. Others believe that it is the environment that many Black males grow up in that creates a desperation that begets lawless activity, that Black communities spawn criminal delinquents.

It is no secret that many African Americans come from communities that are poor and destitute. And considering the theory that extreme poverty often serves as the parent to criminal activity, my research interests have largely been comprised of finding solutions that are intended to address poverty and the country's wealth disparities. Many of my wide-ranging, overarching societal questions have centered on gaining an understanding of how and why so many Black communities have become so poor and poverty-stricken. There is no conversation about a proverbial barrel without addressing the country's long-standing wealth and income disparities.

CHAPTER FOUR
BLACK COMMUNITIES:
ARE THEY POOR AND DESTITUTE BY DESIGN?

*"This...country set you down in a ghetto in which, in fact, it
intended that you should perish. "*
James Baldwin

There are no secrets surrounding the wealth disparities that have troubled and continue to trouble America.
White Americans have always exceeded persons of color with
regard to income levels and wealth assets. A recent Pew Research Center report declared that White households claim a
median wealth advantage 18 times that of Latino households
and 20 times that of African American households. In fact, as
a result of the 2008 recession, Latino households went from
a net worth of $18,359 in 2005 to $6,325 in 2009. This drop
represented a 66 percent decrease, the largest decline of any
ethnic group. The report asserts that these wealth gap ratios
are the largest since the government starting acquiring such

data some 30 years ago. The study maintains that these numbers are twice the size of the ratios that existed throughout the two decades that led up to the country's recent recession.[1] The bursting housing bubble is widely understood as the impetus for the economic collapse. More specifically, when the value of American homes began to plummet, the stability of the economy began to come into question. As faith in the American economy began to drastically decline, so did the overall household wealth of people of color. The quintessential symbol of the American Dream—a single-family home—melted away for many Black and Brown families overnight. Perhaps the larger tragedy was the fact that many of these families had just recently started to realize this "Dream" after being systematically barred from it for years before.

According to author and historian Louis Woods, African Americans were once viewed as "undesirable residents" and "dangerous bank investments" by the savings and loan industry. In his thought-provoking 2012 article, "The Federal Home Loan Bank Board, Redlining, and the National Proliferation of Racial Lending Discrimination, 1921-1950," Woods draws our attention to the actions and operations of the Home Owners' Loan Corporation (HOLC), a federal agency established by Congress to address the collapsed housing market of the Great Depression. This loan corporation was governed by the Federal Home Loan Bank Board (FHLBB), an entity also established by Congress to stabilize the floundering American economy. The converging of these two congressionally instituted units created the groundwork for long-term nationwide financing strategies and lending practices. These governmentally authorized bodies designed appraisal methods and lending procedures that deemed entire neighborhoods "dangerous bank investments" and those that resided in them as "undesirable residents." Professor Woods astutely articulates these sentiments in the following excerpt:

> The lasting legacy of the HOLC was its emergency lending practices that saved the dwellings of hundreds of thousands of distressed urban home owners from foreclosure and the residential appraisal scheme it proliferated. The HOLC became the direct lending and appraisal arm of the FHLBB. It used an appraisal technique that analyzed residential neighborhood composition and deemed entire neighborhoods dangerous bank investments whenever undesirable residents inhabited them. The HOLC, under the auspices of the FHLBB, defined undesirable residents as racial or ethnic minorities, or low-income inhabitants. The incorporation of these new "scientific appraisal" standards by the FHLBB influenced national lending policy by disadvantaging entire communities it deemed a hazardous bank investment.[2]

These powerful organizations, operating in tandem, systemically and systematically banished people of color from suitable home ownership. As a result, they forced persons of color into some of the worst living conditions in the country. Race and ethnicity had become such influential factors in determining neighborhood desirability, even African American citizens (doctors, lawyers, professors, politicians) whose income levels exceeded that of many White Americans were seen as "undesirable residents." African Americans, when offered home loans, were presented the "most unattractive home financing terms." Meanwhile, America's White middle class was being established and even expanded through programs like the Federal Housing Act of 1934 (FHA), where the private lending industry was backed by the federal government. Because of FHA's "confidential" city surveys and appraisers' manuals, African Americans and other racial and ethnic minorities were denied full access to the American Dream of home ownership.

Between 1934 and 1962, FHA and the Veterans Administration (VA) financed more than $120 billion worth of new housing real estate. Astonishingly, less than two percent went to families of color. These governmentally sanctioned stipulations served to quarantine African American and low-income households into the most densely-populated and decrepit living conditions with extremely limited livable space—American ghettos. Consequently, and as a result of these discriminatory lending and housing practices, African Americans and other persons of color resided in the country's most "deplorable housing conditions" by the middle of the twentieth century. As a matter of fact, African Americans in 1950 occupied the "worst dwellings" in the nation despite significant employment and salary increases created by the wartime prosperity of the second World War.[3]

Fast-forward to present day, we find many African Americans still living in the country's "worst dwellings." Any attempt to divorce these current conditions from the country's record of discrimination would be intentionally ambigguous, tremendously uninformed and extremely myopic. Poor African American families have not foolishly chosen to live in abject poverty as a result of some twisted form of self-desolation. Neither have they opted for dead-end jobs with dismal pay or poor performing school districts with sub-par learning facilities. Not only are the residual effects of past housing and lending practices liable for the station in which many Black families currently find themselves, the manner in which other significant governmental policies were carried out served to sequester Black progress as well. Several public policies during President Franklin D. Roosevelt's New Deal era and President Harry S. Truman's Fair Deal era were fashioned and subsequently administered in discriminatory ways. Many of these groundbreaking and long-lasting strategies largely excluded people of color.

The Raw Deal

In the 1930s and 1940s, in an effort to resuscitate a country reeling from the wounds of the Great Depression, American politicians put their heads to together to create a number of mechanisms that served to restore America's viability. It was during this era that the GI Bill was established. This bill provided a number of benefits for veterans of the Armed Forces. As well, Social Security was birthed during this time period. Social Security was established mainly to sustain the elderly after retirement, but also served to assist widows and the poor and unemployed. There were also a number of labor laws that surfaced during this era as well that protected workers and promoted unions. These laws and legislations were commonly known as the New Deal during

Roosevelt's administration and the Fair Deal during Truman's administration. Unfortunately, most African Americans were refused the benefits of these programs due to discriminatory practices.

Take Social Security, for example. It was intended to protect citizens from the economic hazards of old age. It also provided citizens a buffer during periods of economic inertia or unemployment. Social Security became the most important social legislation of that day, but Blacks were in large measure excluded. They were disqualified from assistance because the program did not support agricultural workers and domestic servants, and the majority of Blacks fell into these employment categories as a result of being barred from other professions during that era. The outcomes were the same with regard to labor laws. The labor provisions did not make room for domestic and farm workers, thus disregarding scores of Black citizens.

The GI Bill, considered by many scholars as the legislation that created America's middle class, helped millions of veterans to gain jobs, launch businesses, obtain higher education and purchase homes. Though the program assisted a number of African American veterans, it omitted a substantial number due to the country's widespread devotion to racism, mainly because most of the Bill's administrators were Southern politicians who strictly adhered to Jim Crow's demands. The educational component of the program was perhaps most harmful in that Black veterans could not take full advantage of the subsidy as a result of being denied access to "Whites only" educational institutions. Many Black veterans were forced to attend historically black colleges and universities (HBCUs) only. Though most HBCUs were stellar institutions, space and facilities were limited, causing a considerable number of Black veterans to be turned away. Ira Katznelson, in *When Affirmative Action was White*, concisely sums up the end results of the era:

> The exclusion of so many [B]lack Americans from the bounty of public policy, and the way in which these important, large-scale national programs were managed, launched new and potent sources of racial inequality. The federal government, though seemingly race-neutral, functioned as a commanding instrument of [W]hite privilege.[4]

This era marked a time of unprecedented aid and service to a generation of people striving for the fundamental accoutrements of life. Many people were set on pathways that would forever alter their family's trajectory. Many individuals were able to obtain the educational gains that would afford them the jobs and income that would set them on a path of prosperity that sustains their families until today. The country's educational landscape, workforce customs and social welfare system would be established and strengthened during this era. If slavery established America's economy, this time period certainly resurrected it after a brief setback. Lives were forever changed as a result of the legislative provisions of these years. Just as the stipulations of this era set a prosperous path for some individuals, in many ways, it did the opposite for others. Many Black families were set on a course of poverty and strife as a result of their exclusion from these federally sanctioned subsidies. We cannot continue to propose solutions to our contemporary problems without giving full consideration to these truths. African Americans were systemically and systematically locked out. From my vantage point, these national misfortunes took place during a time not so long ago. Just as we get a glimpse of the future by gazing into the eyes of our children, we are reminded of former times through the lives and experiences of our parents and grandparents, of a past that's not so distant.

A Not So Distant Past

Let's take a look at how recent history really is; I will use my mother and father as examples. My dad was born in 1941 and my mother in 1942, which may seem like a long time ago. But, when I reveal that they are now in their mid-seventies and still living very active lives, you may conclude that 1941 and 1942 are actually pretty recent. When I juxtapose their years of birth with the year slavery was abolished, 1865, it may feel like the dates are light years apart. But there is really only a 76 and 77 year gap, respectively, between the occasions of my parents' birth and the abolition of slavery. This actually represents a short amount of time, especially considering that many people routinely live longer than 76 or 77 years.

Taking these facts into consideration, there is no doubt that my mother and father came into contact with slavery; not directly, but through other family members who had come into contact with slavery. Both my parents were raised by their grandmothers, who both were born in 1904: my mother's grandmother on May 1, 1904, and my father's grandmother on August 10, 1904. My great-grandmothers almost certainly came into contact with those who had actually lived through slavery, because they were born a mere 39 years after slavery's conclusion. Any elderly person in their lives would have surely been familiar with slavery. My family is from the coast of South Carolina, the Deep South, from one of the primary port cities where most enslaved Africans entered the country.

History books record that in 1850, my hometown of Georgetown, South Carolina, consisted of approximately 20,000 people. And, astoundingly, 90 percent of those people were enslaved Africans.[5] I understand that all African Americans are not direct descendants of enslaved Africans, but the likelihood that my family is the offspring of those Africans is extremely high. Thus, I can say with relative certainty that my great-grandparents touched the hands of slavery. And, bearing in mind their close contact with my parents, I can declare that my mother and father experienced some of the accompaniments of slavery through their grandmothers. Taking this a step further, I can say that I experienced, through my great-grandparents, grandparents and parents, many of the remnants of slavery. I am sure of it.

My great-grandmothers both lived well into old age. My mother's grandmother lived to the ripe old age of 91; she passed away in 1995. My father's grandmother died in 2006 at 102. My brother, cousins and I spent many days with both of my great-grandmothers working in their gardens. They both had gardens on their property; one lived in a rural community about 10 miles outside of town limits, and the other lived in the middle of town. When we were not in their gardens, we were shellin' beans, snappin' peas or shuckin' corn from those gardens, all the while listening to them hum old songs or share stories of days gone by. I vividly remember my great-grandmother, Florie, my dad's grandmother, working well into old age as a domestic for a White family in my hometown. The remnants of an old era died slowly in South Carolina. So, for me, there is no denying the direct and pervasive impact of history on modern times.

Considering the scope and effects of slavery on modern life, we must also recognize the propinquity and residual influences of the New and Fair Deals on contemporary circumstances. If we acknowledge the residue of slavery on the present day, then surely we must accept the more recent effects of the 1930s, '40s and '50s. Though many of the eras' tactics were covert, the impacts are long-lasting. Perhaps the camouflage of their dispersal has contributed to the potency of their results. It is sometimes challenging to pinpoint history's impact on the happenings of today. But, in order to truly assist a significant number of people of color as they claw for survival, we must move away from an incessant reliance on pathology as the cause for despair.

It is not an ordained fact that Black and Brown people, en masse, should live in abject poverty or in neighborhoods wrought with gloom and doom. This mindset contributes to the fact that, in spite of countless years of work to level the playing field, the field remains extremely uneven. We have not delved deep enough into the vestiges of history in our efforts to address the shortcomings of the present. You and I did not determine the neighborhood or the home our parents brought us to at the time of our birth. We must resolve in our collective psyche that history played an important role in that determination. When history is truly considered, we discover that the winners' circle has not been drawn wide enough, it has not even come close to including a wide enough array of individuals. An honest reflection on the past will also cause us to conclude that it was a collective effort that has propelled America into what it is today. Those who have realized a semblance of success have done so with the help of others. I lament the notion of a "self-made" man or women. No one makes themselves; people need people. We must help each other. Our aim as a country should be that of collective aspiration. The country's goal should be to help ALL of its citizens prosper. And, considering that many scholars are predicting that by the year 2050, the United States will be a country where people of color are the majority,[6] we must quickly do away with our deep-seated anxieties around matters of race. I sincerely believe that America will do and be much better, if everyone is marching in the same direction. Some believe that America's poor can serve as the front-runners of this movement toward shared prosperity and sustainability.

The Least of These

Author and entrepreneur John Hope Bryant believes that the solution to America's economic well-being lies in how it has defined poverty and how it treats those who are impoverished. Bryant believes that a shift in how we view poverty can serve as the linchpin for a better tomorrow. Those who are poor are not only, in large measure, blamed for the condition in which they find themselves, but are often treated as less than human because of their circumstances. The end result is a people void of hope and negated the chance to educate themselves or their offspring. What is left are communities, many teeming with immense, but untapped talents. This creates, in some, a sense of hopelessness and despair. Bryant believes that "the most dangerous person in the world is a person with no hope." Bryant states further that "over time, people, cultures and communities respond internally to how they are treated externally. Tell someone they aren't valuable or important and, in time, far too many of them begin to believe it."[7]

Might this be what has happened and is still happening in most major cities in this country? Could this be the cause of the immeasurable blood-shed we have witnessed in cities like Chicago and New Orleans? We must provide more opportunities for poor communities to operationalize their talents and intelligences. Many of our communities simply lack hope. The viability of the entire country is at stake. When we are given the opportunity to hope, we navigate barriers better. Hopeful people are not those who are void of experiencing despair, but are those who are provided the opportunity to anticipate problems. Hopeful people are those who, when problems are foreseen, devise plans to address those problems. This is entrepreneurship. I have heard a number of my mentors say that necessity is the predecessor to discovery. I have taken this to mean that when people are given the opportunity and tools to address their own needs, the outcomes are often lucrative, not only for their specific communities, but for our larger community as well. Economists believe this to be the potential instigator of a booming economy. When we are afforded the opportunity to dream, work and earn money, we spend money, which ultimately drives the economy. Bryant, in *How the Poor Can Save Capitalism,* explains it this way:

> Consumers—not businesses or government—power the bulk of our massive economy, with fully 70 percent of the economy dependent on consumer spending. This means that you and I are driving the largest economy in the world, by purchasing everything from iced cappuccinos to ice shovels, from gas to put in our cars to the cars themselves. Sustained economic growth and the fortunes of the other 30 percent of the economy represented by businesses and government, therefore, depends on the economic vibrancy of ordinary consumers, most of whom are not wealthy...these ordinary Americans are much more reliable spenders than the wealthy; the bottom 80 percent of the American workforce spends 90 percent of its income, whereas the wealthiest 1 percent spends only 49 percent. The average American cannot afford not to spend the bulk of his or her paycheck on the basic necessities of living, but the rich simply make too much to spend it all.[8]

America's economic vibrancy can only return through an engaged and educated citizenry. The country's very survival is dependent upon a widespread embracing of our poor and diverse communities. There are demographic changes afoot that we have not seen before, and our educational system is on the front lines of these changes. Educators, in many respects, are the first segment of society responsible for establishing the trajectory of the arc that will eventual enclose the aforementioned winners' circle. But, in order to draw the circle wide enough to include the needs of a more diverse student populace and to avoid replication of past societal missteps, educators must be equipped with the tools to relate to their students and families of color, many who bring a variety of experiences and backgrounds to the learning environment. Any and all work done in the effort to prepare educators to receive the influx of students of color must begin with an examination of the demographic make-up of the country's teaching force.

Though there has been a slight shift in the K-12 teaching populace in recent years, teachers who classify themselves as White still make-up the largest portion of the teaching force. In 2011, Caucasian teachers accounted for 84 percent of all teachers nationwide. Teachers of Latin American origin are the fastest growing group in K-12 schools, but still only constitute 6 percent of all public school teachers. African American teachers make-up about 7 percent of all teachers, while 4 percent of teachers classify themselves as "other." In contrast to the teaching population, recent predictions suggest that as early as 2020, Caucasian students will only be the majority in public schools by a few percentage points, and by 2026, students of color will make up 70 percent of all public school students across the country. Interestingly, students of color already make up the majority of public school students in eleven states: Alabama, Arizona, California, Florida, Hawaii, Louisiana, Maryland, Mississippi, Nevada, New Mexico, and Texas.[9] With teacher and student populations changing at starkly different rates, it is imperative that Caucasian teachers become better prepared

105

to teach diverse student populations. Not only should these teachers be well-versed in their subject matter, they must be equipped to confront the trappings of race and racism.

Education researchers Maya Kalyanpur and Beth Harry suggest that educators exercise cultural reciprocity in their dealings with students and families of color. Cultural reciprocity, a modification of cultural competency, demands a standard that respects and embraces the cultural perspectives and customs that families of color bring to their learning environment. It also mandates that educators willfully share a school's culture with those same families. Cultural reciprocity calls for constant introspection on the part of teachers and administrators that promotes a willingness to reflect upon the often unquestioned aspects of school culture, aspects such as the sometimes incomprehensible academic jargon that often objectifies that which should not be objectified.[10] When specifically looking at higher education and its ability to accommodate change, Professor Samuel Betances describes the phenomenon as such:

> For the first time in the history of colleges and universities, educators have to do what no previous generation of their peers had ever done before: educate learners who are members of the dominant society along with those who are not...educate those who are blessed with a vast network of supporters who provide resources to help them complete academic projects and who eagerly assist in removing socio-political/economic hurdles so they can climb to the top of their class, along

with those who are not blessed with such support; educate those for whom completing post-secondary, higher educational requirements, and earning degrees form part of their rich family history, along with those for whom it does not; educate those whose cultural heritage/interest/racial group identities are positively affirmed in our racially stratified society, along with those whose are not.....The reason higher education must succeed in educating learners with and without all the pluses noted above has to do with demographic changes. Simply put, the demographic base available to colleges and universities to recruit and develop the talent for professional leadership needed by our public and private institutions has been altered forever.

Without inclusive and educated work teams at all levels of our organizations, our nation will not remain productive and competitive in the global economy. Therefore, differences in the fabric of our society must be embraced, not shunned. We must see differences as opportunities to grow in our collective purposes rather than to shrink from our collective expectations. We must practice deliberate inclusivity. We must implement diversity processes as a strategy to unleash the full potential of all the members in our diverse workforce.[11]

Perhaps the most important aspect of our work to include historically excluded groups into the fabric of American life, lies in how we describe them. Instead of continuing to refer to people of color as "minorities," the narrative should and must be changed to "emerging majority groups."[12] This semantic change accounts for the aforementioned demographic changes the country is currently experiencing. As well, the word "minority", for some, has morphed into something totally different from its true meaning. This is made evident by phrases like, "by the year 2050, the United States will be majority-minority,"[13] which is intended to describe the occasion when people of color will become the majority. When people of color become the majority, we will be just that—the majority. I have always taken issue with being described as a minority. There are very few things that are minor about human life. And in America, ethnicity surely hasn't been a minor issue. Yes, people of color are the minority with regard to population numbers, but when we are described as "the minority," the phrase seems to be addressing a sentimentality the stretches beyond quantitative principles. It seems to have morphed into an issue of value or worth and has now become synonymous with inferiority. The semantic change that I describe above is not only needed but warranted. In order to continue to educate individuals, many whom are first-generation Americans and/or first-generation college students, educators must commit themselves to life-long learning. "Educators must become relentless readers"[14] of literature that seeks to address the needs of the historically underserved.

I believe that true education occurs with the discovery of self. Thus, 21st century educators must be prepared to help students discover themselves in places that have not, historically, included people that look like them. It is pretty hard to find oneself in a place where you (collectively) have not previously existed. This is especially true when we look at higher education in America. American colleges and universities have, largely, been upper-and middle-class dwellings, controlled by the hidden rules of those groups, relegating individuals from poor and underserved communities to the margins of campus. Situations and scenarios like this can be successfully navigated, but not without the assistance of caring adults and mentors. These caring adults and mentors must arrive at an understanding that many of the attributes that these students bring to campus, though different from those found in upper-and middle-class communities, are rooted in aptitude and intelligence.

At present, however, there is a chasm that exists between students who come from poor and underserved communities and their educators. They both hold pessimistic views toward each other. Educators are pessimistic about the intelligence and ability levels of underserved students, and students are pessimistic about their teachers' compassion, commitment and competency to reach and ultimately teach them. We must also do away with our preconceived notions of what constitutes intelligence. We must work to eradicate the widespread but, tacit belief that intelligence is both a fixed and a built-in concept. To the contrary, intelligence is a malleable concept that can be shaped by energy and effort.

We must ultimately understand that an inclusive society enhances society as a whole. Meaningful interactions with individuals from various backgrounds and perspectives foster growth for all and especially for those who come from culturally homogenous environments. Our upper-and middle-class students can learn the lessons of "productive struggle" that underserved students, no doubt, bring to the table. And our underserved students can learn the language of the class-based hidden undercurrents that power many of America's institutions.

President Lyndon B. Johnson broached this very topic during the commencement address at Howard University's graduation ceremony in June 1965, 100 years after Lincoln's Emancipation Proclamation. President Johnson started his address with an examination of the very notion of emancipation itself. He, specifically, asserted the perspective that emancipation was simply not enough to elevate poor people of color out of the clutches of oppression. He solicited opportunity on their behalf. Johnson extended the following thoughts with regard to the notion of freedom and opportunity:

> But freedom is not enough. You do not wipe away the scars of centuries by saying: Now you are free to go where you want, and do as you desire, and choose the leaders you please. You do not take a person who, for years, has been hobbled by chains and liberate him, bring him up to the starting line of a race and then say, "you are free to compete with all the others," and still justly believe that you have been completely fair. Thus, it is not enough just to open the gates of opportunity. All our citizens must have the ability to walk through those gates. This is the next

and the more profound stage of the battle for civil rights. We seek not just freedom but opportunity.[15]

He went on to specifically address the needs of poor people of color in juxtaposition to the gains that upper-and middle-class Whites had long experienced, and some middle class Blacks had made:

> But for the great majority of Negro Americans—the poor, the unemployed, the uprooted, and the dispossessed—there is a much grimmer story. They still, as we meet here tonight, are another nation. Despite the court orders and the laws, despite the legislative victories and the speeches, for them the walls are rising and the gulf is widening.

> Here are some of the facts of this American failure.

> • Thirty-five years ago the rate of unemployment for Negroes and [W]hites was about the same. Tonight the Negro rate is twice as high.
> • In 1948, the 8 percent unemployment rate for Negro teenage boys was actually less than that of [W]hites. By last year that rate had grown to 23 percent, as against 13 percent for [W]hites unemployed.

- Between 1949 and 1959, the income of Negro men relative to [W]hite men declined in every section of this country. From 1952 to 1963 the median income of Negro families compared to [W]hite actually dropped from 57 percent to 53 percent.
- In the years 1955 through 1957, 22 percent of experienced Negro workers were out of work at some time during the year. In 1961 through 1963 that proportion had soared to 29 percent.
- Since 1947 the number of [W]hite families living in poverty has decreased 27 percent while the number of poorer non-[W]hite families decreased only 3 percent.
- The infant mortality of non-[W]hites in 1940 was 70 percent greater than whites. Twenty-two years later it was 90 percent greater.
- Moreover, the isolation of Negro from [W]hite communities is increasing, rather than decreasing as Negroes crowd into the central cities and become a city within a city.

Of course Negro Americans as well as [W]hite Americans have shared in our rising national abundance. But the harsh fact of the matter is that in the battle for true equality too many— far too many—are losing ground every day. [16]

112

Sadly, much of President Johnson's 1965 speech correlates with today's circumstances. African American unemployment rates remain twice that of White American unemployment rates. In fact, it has remained so for the past six decades. When we look at African Americans, ages 16-24, their unemployment rate skyrockets to 22 percent, whereas the national unemployment rate is 5.5 percent. Black family incomes still lag drastically behind White family income, with Black median household income at $34,600 and White median household income at $58,270. A recent report, entitled *The Roots of the Widening Racial Wealth Gap: Explaining the Black-White Economic Divide*, states that between 1984 and 2009, White households added $5.19 of wealth for every dollar increase in income versus only 69 cents wealth increase for every dollar gained in income for Black households. Poverty rates are quite similar, with Black poverty hovering at 27.2 percent and White poverty at 9.6 percent. [17]

We must do something about these dismal figures. First, we must continue to educate the masses that these gaps exist. Again, when you reside in a country that collectively believes that fairness and equality abound, efforts to convince folks otherwise must be both commonplace and frequent. Our commitment to overcome poverty must be widespread. Society as a whole must be made to understand that assistance to and for the poor ultimately helps us all.

Poverty is far more than a lack of income or a shortage of resources; it represents an absence of compassion on the part of those who are in a position to help. Much of our national response to poverty has been a business-as-usual approach. We proceed through life as though hardship and despair are as natural as air and water, that they are just normal aspects of life. I understand that everyone is not going to be a millionaire, but this fact should not justify complete destitution for some in our communities. This very reason is why, I believe, Dr. King transferred his attention to the Poor People's Movement just prior to his death. He understood that, together, the country would be much stronger if it inspired poor people to higher aspirations.

As it stands today, far too many neighborhoods are comprised of blocks and blocks of poor people. In the long run, economists believe these kinds of arrangements cost the country money. These circumstances surely effect the youth in these communities. They end up with a dearth of examples and possibilities for the future. Just as I mentioned in an earlier chapter, I am now an educator largely because I had an abundance of mentors and role models during my formative years. None of them were millionaires, but prosperous in their own way. Our youth need to see their parents and neighbors in positions of sustainable prosperity. Children will be what they see.

CHAPTER FIVE
NOW WHAT?

"Infuse your life with action. Don't wait for it to happen. Make it happen. Make your own future. Make your own hope. Make your own love. And whatever your beliefs, honor your creator, not by passively waiting for grace to come down from upon high, but by doing what you can to make grace happen...yourself, right now, right down here on Earth."
Bradley Whitford

Up to this point, I have laid out a lot of facts about our country's history, of how Europeans first enslaved millions of Africans and then successfully excluded large segments of African Americans from the full benefits that citizenship should have brought them. While I understand these facts of history to be true, I am not implying that African Americans stood by hopelessly, serving as pawns in an all-powerful chess game of White domination. I am not suggesting that we were merely weak-minded imbeciles who lacked the critical thinking skills or the courage to navigate the perils that life in America posed. Because we have been much the opposite; we have been able to survive treacherous conditions.

In opposition to what some early historians believed, slavery did not end because it became an unproductive and antiquated system that yielded poor profit margins. Slavery died because enslaved Africans continually challenged the chains of captivity. Many vehemently and violently defied the shackles of suppression. Those who argue otherwise have yielded to myopic interpretations of what poses, for me, a puzzling paradox. If African Americans were such a pathetic bunch, why did Europeans see such value in us? First, they extracted us from Africa and then spent considerable energy trying to keep us in a subordinate state. One in ten slave voyages experienced major rebellions, and there were hundreds, if not thousands, of revolts on plantations all across America.[1] Some were successful and some not, but unfortunately many were not recorded in our history books, robbing us of the opportunity to revisit the strength and courage that dwells within. I don't want you to misinterpret my words here; slavery and the racism it required to be successful were quite overpowering. Together, they rendered considerable damage to America as a whole. I simply want it to be understood that our enslaved ancestors did something about their circumstances.

Likewise, my inferences up to this point have not been an attempt at saying Black people are the cause for all of the problems we face or that there exists some sort of cultural illness that runs rampant among African American people that drives many of us over the proverbial edge. It is no secret that many of us lead destructive lives, but to suggest that these destructive behaviors are the result of culture or pathology is simply absurd and void of a thorough understanding of American history. But, as powerful as racism has proven to be, I think it would be extremely unwise to suggest that it is such a powerful force that it cannot be defeated. Unfortunately, many of us have become so overwhelmed with the pressures of life and entangled in the tentacles of racism that we have accepted defeat and have blamed mainstream America for our demise. I realize that defeating racism is a daunting task, but it is one, I believe, that can be accomplished. We simply have to learn where to focus our attention and energy.

While I appreciate the notion that complaining about the country's state of affairs has therapeutic value, our complaints alone do very little to change things. As well, any attempt to justify the criminal activity of some among us by pointing to the deeds of mainstream America as the cause would be an exercise in both careless and reckless negligence. It would also represent a rejection of our collective responsibility to take action.

There is no denying that a society has serious flaws when it relegates a significant portion of its citizens to slum-like living conditions and then holds them solely culpable for living in those conditions. It is also quite telling when a society refuses to adequately educate its youth and incarcerates millions more who come from the same underserved communities of color. But, the truth of the matter is, "life ain't been no crystal stair"[2] for lots of people. To highlight the fact that life has been harder for some of us will garner little sympathy on the account of the country's delusional belief in meritocracy. In fact, the reality that some of us live poverty-stricken lives would serve as proof of our inferiority in the minds of many. Stating the truth about our country's past is one thing, but living in a state of perpetual belly-aching is another.

Fortunately, there is a silver lining. We not only have hope, but we now live in an America that is quite different from the America that our parents and grandparents experienced. We can now pursue our dreams with a level of certainty that they can actually come true. You are reading this book because of that fact. We can now aspire to the highest political office in the land and actually expect to have a viable shot at it because we now have an example of someone who has done it. I believe that young African American citizens can truly aspire to be the President of the United States because they now have an example of someone who looks like them who has done it. We have yet to see the impact that President Obama's presidency will have on the lives of youth of color. It enhances the esteem of young Black folk when they see a reflection of themselves standing at the Presidential podium or disembarking from Air Force One or trotting across the White House lawn with his wife and daughters in tow.

In the last few years, there was an interesting photograph floating around the internet of a young African American boy visiting the oval office with his parents. In the photo, President Obama was leaning over to allow the young visitor the opportunity to touch and examine his hair. The picture represents far more than just a curious little boy examining the haircut of the President. I believe that he was confirming that the President was just like him, that not only were their

118

skin complexions similar, but their hair texture felt the same too. I wonder what that little boy will become later in life. I believe that President Obama's presidency is making a huge impact on him and countless other young African American youth. It may not seem very important, but I delight in the fact that the first President that my nine year old son and other African American youth his age are cognizant of is an African American gentleman. He reflects them.

In short, we are not faced with the America our fore-fathers dealt with that made every effort to force them into positions of humiliation and second-class citizenship. Again, I am not suggesting that we are anywhere close to reaching a place where all inequities are swept away. However, I am saying that we have certain economic, social, cultural, pro-fessional and even political opportunities that our forefathers could only dream of having. We have greater involvement in determining our place in the world. These liberties are nowhere close to being absolute, there are still indisputable disadvantages that we face. But, those that we face are not as daunting as those that confronted our elders.

As well, I have mentioned the many consequences of history, not in an attempt to provide excuses as to why Black America cannot succeed. I have done so in an attempt to en-courage an opposite effect. It is my hope to inspire with the information I have offered. I hope that readers find inspira-tion in what we have overcome and accomplished in spite of the many mechanisms that served in opposition to our progress.

I hope to invoke inspiration as opposed to motiva-tion, because I believe that motivation, philosophically, is too temporary. Etymology informs us that the Old English equivalent to "inspire," inspiration's root word, is "enspiren," which means "to fill the mind, heart, etc. with grace, or to prompt or induce." Another translation says "to influence or animate with an idea or purpose." The Latin translation, "inspirare" means "to inflame or blow into."[3] And if you believe the biblical scripture that says, "God formed Man out of dirt from the ground and blew into his nostrils the breath of life. The Man came alive—a living soul," [4] you will understand why I aim to inspire. Anything that happens in the soul has everlasting and eternal affects, thus informing my theory about the permanence of inspiration versus the impermanence of motivation.

I hope the words of this book have a permanent effect on the reader, and inspire the reader to do something about the conditions of Black America. To quote scripture again, "Faith without action is dead."[5] We must resolve to pray as if life's outcomes are up to God, but take action as if life's outcomes are up to us. In order to reverse the many ailments that affect our lives and our communities, we must take action. Below I offer a list of actions I believe we should take as we gain ownership of the things that determine our place in the world.

Find Mentorship. I understand that many African Americans will not have immediate access to viable mentors like I was fortunate to have during my formative years. In those cases, I would advise that a concerted effort is made to find mentorship. Obtaining mentorship is but one of many actions we must take to reverse current circumstances. Mentorship is necessary for the growth and development of social sensitivity, spiritual discernment and personal awareness. Mentorship affiliations can range from formal, where mentee and mentor establish set meeting times and cover planned agenda topics, to informal, where a mentee learns through everyday interactions and observations, keeping in mind that authentic mentorship relationships should consist of a mentee and mentor who mutually acknowledge each other as such.

Though I understand that mentorship bonds are, perhaps, most fruitful when they develop organically through natural interactions, they can also be effective when individuals are paired based on similar backgrounds and interests. Oftentimes sound mentorship is the missing link between a promising existence and a successful one. Mentorship fills the gaps that formal education leaves open. Formal education focuses on the academic only, while mentorship addresses life concerns that take place outside the classroom such as decision-making, dealing with frustrations and disappointments and balancing home life with work life.

Finding a mentor may pose a problem for some because of limited interaction with a person or persons to serve in such roles. But until a mentor is found, it is fine to settle for good role models. Role models are individuals perhaps not known on a personal level, but are individuals admired from a distance. Though I have had great mentors throughout my life, I have also had great role models, people whom I have admired from afar. She or he could be someone working in an industry that is appealing or a person who conducts themselves in a manner the mentee would like to emulate. All in all, we must find someone who can help guide our footsteps through life. This point provides a perfect segue to the next action item.

Be a Mentor. Being part of the village that helps

young people to reach new heights is an important piece in the puzzle of collective progress. When we help a young person to move along their life's journey, we inadvertently help ourselves as these individuals will, one day, be the decision-makers creating public policy that ultimately affects us all, or the healthcare professionals who assist with our medical needs in the future. Mentorship efforts should include individuals that are outside the family circle (i.e., son, daughter, niece, nephew, etc.). While mentoring efforts should naturally include family members, energies should also include those that are not a part of a biological circle. At a base level, being a mentor helps confirm to a mentee that they have access to someone, outside their family circle, who cares about them.

Mentorship has been known to assist young people in a number of impactful ways, to include increased self-esteem, gains in social awareness as well as social acceptance and enhanced academic attitudes and performance. Overall, mentorship is proven to be a beneficial endeavor for all involved parties including the mentors. It is rewarding work.

When taking on the role of mentor, one must understand it is a serious endeavor. As such, a mentor should be prepared for a long-term commitment. To avail oneself to a mentee and then renege on that commitment shortly thereafter could be more detrimental than no commitment in the first place. Many of our young people are already dealing with abandonment issues, so being confronted with yet another could serve as the final hardship for a train headed for derailment. Mentorship relationships should continue until the mentee is ready to take on a mentee of his or her own. As a matter of fact, many mentorship affiliation last informally for a life time. As a seasoned professional, I still check in with my mentors from time to time. As well, many of my mentees still check in with me on an as-needed basis. The job of a leader is to create other leaders, and building leaders takes time.

Get Educated. As an academician, of course I would advise getting educated. But, I am not necessarily talking about formal education only. Again, I believe that true education involves the discovery of self. Thus, I often advise my students that most of their education will take place outside of the college classroom, that they will have to learn how to manage the intangibles of life in order to successfully navigate the tangibles. When fully educated on the vastness of self, a person is then prepared to sincerely embrace all of life's offerings—the good and the bad. It was Ralph Ellison in *Invisible Man* who profoundly declared, "When I discover who I am, I'll be free."[6]

So what does discovery of self look like? It includes a thorough understanding of one's position in and throughout history, not just your time on American soil, but also a reasonable grasp of one's African history. In an ideal world, this would include tracing genealogy back to a specific region in Africa. But if a genealogy study is not possible, begin to position Africa in its rightful place, as the birthplace of humanity. It builds self-esteem to know that our lineage extends to the beginnings of civilization. Arabs, Chinese, Czechs, Finns, Japanese, Russians and Turks all have full access to their classical histories. Likewise, African Americans must refer to ancient African civilizations, like Benin, Djenne, Kush, Ghana, Meroe, Nubia, and Songhay, as we position ourselves as important citizens of the world's population. In fact, the very notion of Black inferiority is more or less a new concept. Were we able to engage the founding fathers of ancient Greece, they would find it silly to even suggest African inferiority, considering that they patterned their entire society after African civilizations.

We must refer to Africa and its ancient civilizations as we raise the topic of Black history. Though extremely pivotal to the world's history, too often we limp back to slavery as the starting point for Black history. Interestingly, there are a number of historians who describe American slavery as the interruption of Black history, using the rationale that the era was not initiated or carried out by Black hands or Black thought, and thus it should not be considered Black history.

Randall Robinson believes that, "No people can live successfully, fruitfully, triumphantly without strong memory of their past, without reading the future within the context of some reassuring past, without implanting reminders of that past in the present."[7] All in all, education that includes a discovery of self is a vital part of life. It affords us better futures; it allows us to be free.

Upon entering the school our daughter attended back in Nashville, above the help desk hung a quote by the Greek Philosopher Epictetus that said, "Only the educated are free." Even as an educator, I was slightly offended when I first noticed the quote. What about my grandparents and great-grandparents, who were essentially exiled from a good education? Take my grandfather for example, I remember him learning to read and write around the same time I was learning to read and write. What about my father, who stopped-out of high school in the eleventh grade? What about my love ones who did not go to college? What about them?

After analyzing the quote more thoroughly, I realized the quote was simply saying that those who have a good understanding of themselves are free. Further, those who are educated are free to enjoy the many options that life affords. When someone is educated, life doesn't always dictate to them; they can determine some of life's conclusions. There is a major caveat though. This newfound education/freedom is not only for the few, or the privileged. Similar to the notion of leadership, freedom is to be shared with others.

Let's use the story of Harriet Tubman as an example. She acquired freedom and soon after realized that she did not want freedom just for herself. She pioneered a system that created freedom for countless others. Get free, to help others to get free. And don't let school get in the way of education as we strive for freedom. While school definitely plays a part in education, it is not the only place that holds information. Knowledge can be found anywhere; we simply have to acquire it.

Tap into your will power. The will of the human heart and mind is powerful beyond measure. There are countless stories of people who willed themselves to succeed or willed themselves to survive through bad situations. In fact, one of those persons, quite frankly, could be you. You may have withstood the onslaught of years of doubt; the doubt of others or even self-doubt. Maybe you have survived the slum-like living conditions I described throughout this book. Or, maybe you are a cancer survivor or a wounded veteran or a widow or a widower. Whatever you overcame, you did it. Why stop now? Continue to will what you want.

Because of my early years playing football, I am still

a huge fan of the game. I am always particularly interested in how teams and players motivate—or should I say inspire—themselves to win games. I think that their individual and collective *will* serves a major role in their winnings. We often hear sports commentators talk about a player's *will* to win. I believe we saw this phenomenon at work during the 2012 NFL season. The Baltimore Ravens, an unexpected contender, won the Super Bowl that year. I believe they won, largely, because of the *will* of one man, Ray Lewis. Much like other champions, Lewis's *will* to win was so strong it became contagious. His *will* transferred to his teammates, becoming the entire team's *will*. I believe that the human *will* is just that powerful.

Another case of human *will* is that of Earvin "Magic" Johnson. If you were around in 1991 when the announcement was made that Magic had contracted HIV, you probably joined most of the country in doubting his survival. We heard him say that he was going to beat the virus, but we didn't believe that he could or would. That was 25 years ago, and Magic is still alive and doing very well. I realize that Mr. Johnson is blessed with resources to afford the best medical care around, but I also know that his *will* to live has kept him alive. We have heard him say so on countless occasions. He has often referenced a strong *will* to live, coupled with surrounding himself with optimistic people who promote life. There are many experts, scholars and healthcare professionals who believe that illness is the manifestation of *dis-ease* in the interaction between the mind and the soul, also known as the *will*. So, when we intentionally coordinate the energies of the mind and soul, we can achieve the seemingly impossible. "Up, you mighty people, achieve what you WILL!"[8]

126

Live by a mantra. Or live by several mantras. The last line of the preceding paragraph is a mantra that I recite to myself from time to time. "Up, you mighty man, achieve what you will!" I used a variation of this mantra to inspire the young men of the 100 KINGS Program as well. I have, in years past, written my mantras down on Post-it notes and left them scattered around my house and office. You have to remind yourself of who you are and what you are capable of doing sometimes. Here are a few that I have used throughout the years: "Life is for the living, so I'm living it to the fullest." "I am progressing toward my goals with clear vision and purpose!" These next two are adopted from Coach's quotes: "If life is a game, then I'm playing to win," "I can hit life's curve balls and sliders, too!" My wife always says, "If you stay ready, you don't have to get ready."

Have fun creating your own mantras to live by. Some may say that we are foolish, and that mantras don't pay the bills. But, they can serve to encourage you and others along the way. I believe that those who doubt the power of mantras live by unspoken ones. Their mantras simply may not be as positive.

Be Optimistic. Optimism is defined as the disposition or tendency to look on the more favorable side of events or conditions, or to expect the most favorable outcomes. Another word for optimism is hopefulness. Dr. Shane Lopez, in his extremely inspiring publication, *Making Hope Happen*, believes that hope can propel us toward better lives and even better health. He described hopeful people as those who comport their thoughts and behaviors in an effort to create successful lives for themselves and others.

Hope—more so than I.Q., income levels, grades, or

even test scores—determines how successful a college student will become. Hopefulness and optimism are attributes that "correlate positively with health and even longevity." Optimistic people are those who understand that the present and future are connected through behavior. Hopeful people are individuals who grasp the notion that not only do obstacles and barriers exists, but they also recognize that they are equipped with the tools to successfully navigate those obstacles and barriers. And, perhaps the most interesting quality about hope is the fact that it can be a learned behavior. Learning to be hopeful is simply a matter of carving out time to, "visit your future self." Dr. Lopez encourages us to engage in thought experiments that allows for positive vision forecasting.[9]

For example, when purchasing a vehicle, we typically carve out time to go and test drive vehicles we are interested in buying. Not only do we test drive vehicles, many of us spend a considerable amount of time researching prospective vehicles. Sometimes, we even informally interview perfect strangers when they are driving a vehicle we are interested in buying. We should engage in similar exercises as we navigate the vicissitudes of life. We must make it common practice to inquire of those living the lives we want to lead. We must spend time imagining the space, be it physical, financial, emotional or spiritual, that we would like to occupy. This must be a serious endeavor; just as we carve out time to eat, exercise and sleep, so too must we value our time to dream.

Dream Big. There will come a time in your life when you realize that the dreams that you have had for your life have been too small. Remember when we were kids our dreams seem to have had no boundaries? Somewhere along life's journey, we lost the ability to dream big. Adulthood has caused many of us to give up on our dreams. Admittedly, some of our dreams as kids were a bit unrealistic, but some were excitingly unrealistic. I have heard some individuals (i.e., Actor Will Smith and Motivational Speaker Les Brown) theorize that our dreams should be slightly unrealistic. That our personal vision statements should include concepts and ideas that are far-reaching.

Imagine for a second the absolute absurdity of the dream the Wright Brothers championed. Their dream was to fly. Envision the strange stares they no doubt received from friends, family and strangers when they revealed their dream. I would imagine it was difficult to share such a dream with others, considering the sheer impracticality of it. But lo and behold, airplanes are now as much a part of human life as bicycles. In fact, there may be some individuals who have never learned to ride a bike, but enjoy the convenience of flying on a regular basis. The Wright Brothers dreamed big.

There are countless others who carried to fruition what, I am sure, seemed like ridiculous dreams when first revealed. I can think of more than a few dreams that would have seemed outlandish at the onset: the telephone, automobile, computer, internet, camera, radio, etc. Simply because they are so practical today does not mean they were no less impractical yesterday. So, continue to dream big and make sure that they are excitingly unrealistic. They just may come true.

Trust the Spirit within you. All of the world's holy books were written by people. In truth, part of the reason they are so revered is because they were written by people.

We often triumphantly declare that these people were divinely inspired by God. These spiritually connected humans received divine inspiration from God himself, and wrote these extremely revered books of life, love and light. I believe these proclamations to be true, that God inspired these holy writings. Similarly, I believe that divine inspirations still occur. God continues to inspire. Many of the practicalities of life, some I mentioned in the preceding paragraphs, were divine inspirations. Because they are so common, we sometimes fail to recognize the miracle that they represent.

I spoke of the airplane earlier and of how it may have been viewed as impractical initially. Because of its prevalence today, we now fail to realize the complete miracle that it epitomizes. On a flight a few years back, I was fortunate to sit beside an off duty pilot. He had just finished a day of flying and was hopping a ride back to his home base for a few days of rest and relaxation. I took the opportunity to inquire about the science that ultimately causes an aircraft to take-off, remain in flight and then land. He gave me a crash course on aerodynamics. He talked about the lift-to-drag ratio and the speed at which the aircraft had to accelerate down the runway and so forth. I understood the premise of the theory, but walked away more in awe of the miracle it takes for airplanes to fly than in the science of aerodynamics. At the end of day, I relished the fact that mankind had created this extremely convenient means of transportation.

I am sure, by now, you see where I am going with my line of reasoning. The spirit that lives in you created the world in which we live. In point of fact, it created you. And you are a reflection of that creator. The fact that we serve as major players in the human reproduction process confirms, for me, that we are mini creators ourselves. Honor the spirit within. You are extremely powerful. You must trust and believe that you are.

Honor your time. Just as I have encouraged you to trust and honor the spirit within you, I also encourage you to honor the time that you have been given. Our time on Earth is a finite commodity and thus will eventually run out. Don't make it a practice to abuse time or take it for granted, because it is not promised. It is also certainly unadvisable to abuse or take someone else's time for granted, so if someone is gracious enough to give you a portion of their time, please honor their sacrifice. Make every effort to show up to your engagements on time. Whether they are obligatory or leisure activities, please honor them with prompt attention. There are very few things more disrespectful than the abuse of time, yours or someone else's.

There has been an age old debate about the value of time versus money. Some would like to believe that money trumps time. I have come to the conclusion that time definitely carries more value than money. I believe this to be so because there are many structures in our society that make it true, our system of labor and wage being one that clearly makes it so. At our jobs, we typically exchange our time for money. Especially for hourly workers, the more time you give, the more money you earn. Because of this, I have concluded that time is more valuable since we cannot do the inverse with our money. We cannot exchange money for more time. It doesn't matter your monetary assets; you cannot purchase more than 24 hours in a day or more than 60 minutes in an hour or more than 60 seconds in a minute. Though our financial resources may afford us world class healthcare that can help to extend our lives in some cases, when our time is up, it's up. No amount of money can extend life beyond that set moment, so honor your time.

Keep record of what you're grateful for. During my senior year in high school, I decided to compete for the honor to represent my school as Mr. Georgetown High. As participants in the pageant, we were required to come up with a personal motto or slogan. My motto was borrowed from a really popular Bobby McFerrin song from that era, "Don't Worry, Be Happy!" During the question and answer portion of the ceremony, the host asked me the following question: "Suppose you have just survived a bad accident and awaken to find that you have sustained serious injuries, so much so that you will have to learn to talk and walk again. What would you have to be happy for" My response was, "My life." I won the honor to represent my school as Mr. Georgetown High, but I later realized that my response could have been a bit more in depth. Though I believe my response helped me to win, there were a litany of additional details I could have mentioned as things to be grateful for, even under such difficult circumstances.

In recent years, the field of positive psychology has reported that the act of giving thanks has social, psychological and physical benefits. The benefits of giving thanks range from decreases in physical illnesses, heightened feelings of happiness among adults and children as well as the ability to sleep better. Perhaps the most popular method to record gratefulness comes in the form gratitude journaling. Some psychologists, in their efforts to treat patients suffering from depression, have encouraged gratitude journaling. Patients are encouraged to record things they are grateful for once or twice a week. Dr. Robert Emmons, the world's foremost authority on the science of gratitude, suggests that gratitude journal entries be brief and should strive for depth over breadth. He believes that gratitude exercises should focus on the people you are grateful for more so than things. He encourages an approach that reflects on what life would be like without certain blessings rather than simply tallying a list of inanimate objects you are grateful to possess.[10] Ultimately, there is no right or wrong way to count your blessings; it is just imperative that you count them.

Ask for and accept help when you need it. As I have previously stated, people need people, so asking for and receiving help are natural components of life. In fact, I contend that asking for help is one of the most critical aspects of a successful life. When we forge ahead into unfamiliar territory without seeking the assistance of others, we run the risk of injurious outcomes. Trust me, every successful person you know has received help along the way.

When you ask for help, you are also benefitting the person who has been asked. Seeking help is an inadvertent declaration of value and validation of the person being asked. In most cases, the person being asked receives the gesture as an indication of respect. Asking for help also sends the message that it is, indeed, okay to do so. Especially when in positions of leadership, your asking for help gives others permission to do the same. Cultural norms are often set when a leader is seen asking for help, particularly in the workplace. Employees receive their cues both verbally and non-verbally from their leaders, so requesting help can be made into a workplace normative.

As part of focus group discussions that were held at

the conclusion of the 100 KINGS Program, we asked the participants a series of questions pertaining to the notion of asking for and receiving help. When asked the question, "Is it manly to receive help when you need it?" one of the young man said the following: "Of course it's manly. That's what a man does! Why not ask for help and receive help, when you need it?" Another young man said the following: "A man is someone who gets ahead in life and always takes the next step. And if you're needing help with something and won't ask for help, then you don't move to the next level. It's the difference between being arrogant and humble when you refuse to receive help. Men are humble and they realize when they need something, they get it." Here, the student emphatically equates manhood with the gesture of asking for help. It is a profoundly powerful analysis in my estimation.

Don't delight in failure. I think that we sometimes romanticize the notion of failure. We often give failure more credit than it deserves. Throughout life we have heard quotes like: "Success is not built on success, it's built on failure," "We are successful, when we're not afraid to fail" or "Success starts with failure."

I realize that some may say I am being a bit too literal here. Others may even say I am overlooking the fact that failure, in these cases, is being positioned as a teaching tool. But learning the lessons of failure is futile if we don't put them to use. Yes, failure is an important piece on the road to success, but I believe that our actions after a failure is the driving force of success. It takes courage to try after a failure. So, let's fall in love with the actions after a failure as opposed to failure alone.

I would agree that failure provides great life lessons.

Failure often spawns clarity of thought; we sometimes see things a bit clearer from the vantage point of lying flat on our backs. Failure can also help us find our true supporters. Those that stay through tough times are valuable assets. Also, creativity is often the outcome of failure. The imagination is frequently provoked further after endeavors we thought to be our best work failed. Even resilience is often found as a result of failure. But, it is perseverance, not failure, that win races.

Embrace Change. I am sure that you have heard the cliché, "Change is the only constant in life." Well, it is! There are things that have changed about you since you sat down to read this book. The human body, the world, technology, the universe and everything in between is in a state of incessant change. Imagine if none of us changed after birth. I suspect that human life would die out without change. As a matter of fact, I know it would. Life is evolution, and evolution is life. And in most cases, change equates to growth. Thus, we must learn to embrace it.

I understand that change is sometimes a scary endeavor. The uncertainty of change can be nerve-racking at worst and unsettling in the least. Though change is often treated as an imposter in our lives, change is inevitable and ever-present. The good news, however, is that we are good at adapting to change whether we realize it or not. We simply have to train ourselves to embrace that notion.

The first step in training ourselves to embrace change, ironically, deals with acknowledging and accepting our fear of change at the outset. If we are honest with ourselves, it is not change itself that causes trepidation; it is typically our emotional response to change that causes consternation. Our emotional reaction to change renders us ineffective in dealing with it. We must, first, resolve that we have unpleasant feelings about change. Getting real about our feelings has an empowering affect. Ultimately, the problem does not necessarily lie in having a visceral response to change. Troubles exacerbate when we don't express those feelings appropriately and authentically. In the end, we must welcome the wisdom that change, no doubt, brings. Life is at times improbable and definitely impermanent. The quicker we accept these truths, the better. Change cannot be seen or positioned as an enemy. Change is a wise friend who offers great advice.

Expand your boundaries. Sometimes easier said than done, this action item calls for us to step out of our comfort zones. Our comfort zones can, sometimes, foster attitudes of learned apathy, where fear and apprehension come together to serve as a prison; however, some have persuaded themselves that these comfort zones provide security. Yet, others are preoccupied and encapsulated by what Earl Shorris describes as a "surround of force". The forces of poverty, hunger, isolation, illness, police brutality, crime, abuse, racism and countless other stressors all converge to create an enclosure that paralyzes progress. Many have very little, if any, time to think about much else other than their immediate circumstances. They are surely not in positions to engage in the political. Political, "not in the sense of voting in elections, but in the way Thucydides used the word: to mean activity with other people at every level, from the family to the neighborhood to the broader community."[11]

Shorris, a noted author and humanitarian, in an attempt to help a group of poor urbanites expand their boundaries, designed a free course around the humanities. His approach included the study of human constructs and concerns, which he believes have been the structure upon which the elite have educated their off-spring for centuries. He believes that, "the best education for the best is the best education for us all." He structured the course with the intent to provide students the opportunity to engage in meaningful reflection. The curriculum included prose and poetry, art history, logic, philosophy and American history, all taught by full professors from some of the top institutions in the country. Again, he believes that humanities courses are the "foundation for getting along in the world, for thinking, for learning to reflect on the world instead of just reacting to whatever force is turned against you."[12] This line of reasoning is what a liberal arts education entails. It, ideally, creates in students the foundations for critical thought. Through an appreciation of poetry, art and history, an overall appreciation for humanity can be birthed. So, I would advise you to seek ways to expand your boundaries. I realize that the circumstances of life may serve as obstacles to such an endeavor, but your expanded perspective may help you find some of the solutions to those circumstances. In many instances, you cannot afford not to seek expansion. Mankind, when afforded the opportunity to engage in the contemplative, not only will it find solutions to some of the world's problems; it may also find God.

Practice Empathy. I once heard someone define maturity as "the desire to be responsible for another life." If this definition is true, the ability to empathize must accompany this desire for such responsibility. Being responsible for another life means that you would have to, in many cases, see life through the eyes of that individual, which is, in essence, the definition of empathy. I believe that empathy is one of the most important life skills to acquire. But it is, indeed, a skill that must be learned. It starts with learning to listen, which is a universal skill that can help in all aspects of life. Listening should be done with the intent to understand. Empathy requires that you listen in a way that seeks to grasp the motivation of the speaker; that attempts to take into consideration the life experiences that have led an individual to his or her worldview.

Empathy also requires transparency. We, at times, must reveal our truest selves to others as they attempt to make sense of life's fluctuations. The various situations and circumstances that we have overcome can serve to inspire others as they trek through similar conditions. Our collective liberation could, very well, reside within each other.

Empathy must not include any hint of judgment. We must withhold judgment of others as they tread life's ripples. Especially in a larger context, we must refrain from judging others when their actions contradict those that we have taken or would have taken if their situation had been ours. "Until you have walked a mile in someone shoes, don't rush to judge his or her actions." Empathy calls for an emotional intelligence that discerns others' states of emotion, and not only understands their various perspectives, but also identifies with them.

Stop and enjoy life. A few years ago, I read one of the most powerful books I have ever read in my life. *Life is A Gift: Inspirations from the Soon Departed,* by Bob and Judy Fisher, captures the wisdom of individuals suffering terminal illnesses and living out their last days in hospice care. By the time the book was published, all of its contributors had died.

Their messages were that of love, hope, integrity, family, romance, forgiveness and even regret. Resoundingly, they all hoped for more time to enjoy life.

One woman used some of her children's inheritance, much to their chagrin, and took her entire family to a Florida beach house for a week-long vacation in an effort to create more family memories. Another woman lamented and rejoiced, simultaneously, the fact that she had lived such a wonderful life she didn't want to leave it. A man in his forties, who described himself as a "man's man," spoke of smiling when someone smiles at you and holding another person's hand a bit longer during a hand-shake.

They all, emphatically, talked about relationships as the most important aspects of life. Their nearness to death allowed them to see with crystal clarity. All concluded that most of the things they once deemed important were, in actuality, extremely minute. One of the most profound questions Bob and Judy asked the interviewees was, "What comes next for you?" Most of them used humor to respond or to redirect the question, as death was imminent and dreaming seemed foolish. But, the question is a great one for you and me. "What comes next for us?"[13] As for me, I plan to chase my dreams with vigor, but I'll be sure to stop and enjoy life along the way. I would hate to get to the end of my life and have regrets, though it is likely some of us will. It is incumbent upon us to make every effort not to.

Make the decision that no one owes you anything. Let's agree that you will have to earn your way through life. You are responsible for your own successes and failures. As well, you are not entitled to anyone's generosity. While I believe we should be charitable with the resources we have been afforded, we should refrain from any material expectation of the controls and possessions of others. Dr. Steve Perry would tell us to, "Man up, nobody is coming the save us."[14] A step further, I would say, "Man up, nobody is coming to save us but us." Like countless social and political leaders have said over the years, most recently President Obama, "We are the change we've been looking for." I agree. We have what it takes to help ourselves. In the words of James Brown, "I don't want nobody to give me nothing. Open up the door, I'll get it myself." This is the mentality we must adopt. We simply must do what it takes to make it happen. This line of reasoning may lead you to ask what, then, is "it"?

A few weeks ago, my wife asked me one of those deeply profound questions that resurfaces throughout our lifetime, the questions where you have to stop and really examine the crevices of your heart and mind, sometimes for a day or more. She asked me, "What do you want?" I initially thought she was asking me what I wanted to eat for dinner. She later qualified her question by saying, "No, what do you really want out of life?" In my mind, I immediately thought of the cliché answers like, health and happiness. Don't misunderstand me, I do want those things, but in my heart of hearts, I knew there was more that I wanted out of life. After a day or so of careful contemplation, I concluded that what I really want out of life is self-sufficiency. Not the kind of self-sufficiency that assumes I can go through life alone. As I have said before, people need people. The kind of self-sufficiency I desire includes more than just a cursory influence on the outcomes of my life. It is my desire, not only to affect the overarching trajectory of my life; I want to direct the small pathways as well. So the "it" that I referenced above is, for me, self-sufficiency. I want ownership. I would rather stand tall than live on my knees begging of someone else's resources. I insist upon having a major role in creating the desires of my heart. Like the inspirational last words of an impactful poem I learned during my undergraduate years, "I am the master of fate, I am the captain of my soul."[15]

Never give up. Babe Ruth once said, "It's hard to beat a person who never gives up." I think that our people, African American people, are an example of this way of thinking and living. We have not given up. In spite of centuries of struggle, we have not given up. We have not given up on a country that, for all intents and purposes, has ignored our collective humanity since the first African feet stumbled onto American soil. If this statement seems a bit too harsh, at least concede the fact that when African American life has not been ignored, it has been because we have forced the rest of the country to take notice.

Case in point: The country, as I write these words, is in the middle of serious turmoil. Recently, a Missouri grand jury decided not to indict Officer Darren Wilson after what many have described as the cold-blooded murder of a young unarmed teenager, Michael Brown. A few days after the Missouri grand jury's decision, a New York grand jury decided the same fate for Officer Daniel Pantaleo, who applied an outlawed chokehold to the throat of Eric Garner, resulting in his death. Just days before these two grand jury decisions, young Tamir Rice was gunned down by a Cleveland Ohio police officer, Timothy Loehmann, who had been dismissed from a neighboring police force as a result of being deemed "an emotionally unstable recruit and unfit for duty." Many of the comments surrounding this tragic event start with an ad-

141

monishment of young Tamir for playing with a toy gun in the park. The fact that many of the comments began with what Tamir should have or should not have been doing speaks to an inherent lack of sympathy or even empathy for the twelve-year-old African American boy. It is tantamount to blaming a sexual assault victim for being assaulted. It is equivalent to comments like, "She must have done something to provoke the perpetrator," or "She was dressed rather provocatively." It is quite disturbing to hear such comments when someone has been murdered.

Let's face it, little boys do unwise things sometimes, but those things should not end in their death. Tamir was twelve! There are many things he should and should not have been doing, but the adult in the situation should always carry the brunt of responsibility when interacting with a minor. Officer Loehmann's father came out a few days after the shooting and said that his son had no choice in the situation, that his son took the only option available to him. I strongly disagree. There were a number of different choices Officer Loehmann could have made in an effort to spare young Tamir's life. Unfortunately, he did not choose any of the alternative options, and now gone is another young Black life, far too soon.

A bigger tragedy is that deaths like the aforementioned are not isolated events as evidenced in recent FBI data. Recent data show that White police officers kill Black individuals at a rate close to two killings per week. Between 2005 and 2012, Black deaths occurred on average 96 times out of 400 police related shootings per year. Another alarming detail about these data is the fact that more than 50 percent of the deaths were African American men under the age of 20. Perhaps most alarming is the fact that the data are incomplete as many police departments, like the whole state of Florida, do not submit information.[16]

I am dismayed by these killings. In consideration of all that has been happening around the country with regard to police officers and unarmed African American males, it would seem that police officers would be taking meticulous care NOT to use excessive force. Instead, far too many have fallen prey to the pervasive *criminalblackman* image and seem to have increased their use of excessive force. It seems that Black skin has been weaponized in some way.

I am dismayed further because it appears that as much of the country has become anxious over the many protests and rallies that have erupted around the country exclaiming that "Black Lives Matter", I am concerned that these killings, accompanied by the grand juries' decisions not to indict the involved police officers, have created a tipping point. Malcolm Gladwell, in one of his five bestsellers, *The Tipping Point*, makes the case that ideas and even behaviors such as suicide and homicide can spread like viruses. According to Gladwell, these behaviors can be ushered in by one or two individuals. Others often interpret the actions of these one or two individuals as a license to follow suit.[17] Though I hope that these killings are not some sort of disturbing tipping point, because they have been happening so frequently and across various regions of the country, one is forced to ponder the question.

A recent ProPublica study that corroborates the aforementioned FBI data claims that Black males ages 15-19 hold a 21 times greater risk of getting shot by a police officer than their White counterparts. The report revealed that

Black males are killed at a rate that represents 31.17 per million, while White males represented 1.47 per million.[18] And of course, these numbers do not include the actions of self-appointed neighborhood watchmen like Trayvon Martin's murderer or vigilantes with an aversion to loud music like Jordan Davis's killer. Again, I am hopefully that we are not witnessing an endemic of sorts, though the notion has crossed my mind a time or two.

In spite of these and countless other calamities that have affected the Black community, most African Americans still hold an endearing faith in and love for America. A multitude of Black people would not be out protesting these tragedies if this were not so. Though we have not seen justice steered our way in any widespread manner, we have faith that justice will one day be served. Despite the fact that we have had our hearts broken time and time again, we still believe. Though we have collectively cried out, "How long, Lord, How long?" more than a few times, we still wait faithfully. So, despite all that has transpired, take heart! This is your country too. Never give up on it and never give up the right or the fight for ownership.

In the beginning of this chapter, I positioned a list of action items as tools for the fight against racism. On the surface, these action items may not appear to directly address the causes and symptoms of a racialized society. To the contrary, I believe they do. They represent an attempt to affect change in the lives of those impacted most by our racialized society. African Americans are often encouraged to concentrate our thoughts and efforts on changing ourselves. These action steps are intended to do just that; they have been proposed to arouse thought and ultimately to inspire change.

144

Many of us must change the way we feel about ourselves. In many instances, we have bought—hook, line and sinker—extremely negative descriptions and prescriptions about us. Hopefully, these action items will help to reverse our thoughts and feelings about ourselves. Be mindful, however, that this list of action items is not exhaustive; there are a number of additional measures that must be taken in order to affect change and ultimately defeat racism. These are just a few measures we can take to change perceptions—our own as well as the perception of others.

These action items specifically address our plight in the following ways. When we begin to see ourselves as deserving of *mentorship* and competent to serve as *mentors*, we defeat racism. *Getting educated,* tapping into our *will power* and adopting *positive mantras* to live by certainly can help in this fight. As well, *optimism* and *hopefulness* are surely important supplies to take into battle. Knowing how to *dream big* and *trusting the spirit within you* to achieve those dreams are essentials for the ongoing conflict. In order to be successful in this campaign, we must *honor the precious time* we have been afforded, *keep record of the things we are grateful for* along the way and *ask for help* when we need it. We must shun society's widespread love affair with the *notion of failure,* but learn to *embrace* the constancy of *change.* Our stance against injustice must also involve an *expansion of boundaries* on our part, but we must learn to *empathize* with others who fear such expansions. It may sound counterintuitive to suggest that we find ways to *enjoy life* as we participate in battle, but how else will we recognize the importance of what we are fighting for? And, perhaps even more perplexing, don't expect others who may not exactly understand our dilemma, *to assist or to avail their resources.* We must help ourselves. As we engage in this battle for balance, we must resolve to *never give up.* Giving up would be tantamount to accepting the notion of our inferiority. But ultimately, an internalization of these action items will, in the end, cause a shift in the "crabs in the barrel" mentality. These steps will help us to see value in ourselves. Businessman and author Tom Burrell would say that, "We need to undo the effects of America's propaganda campaign that has masterfully marketed the myth of [B]lack inferiority." That our beliefs about each other are just another cog in the "greatest propaganda campaign of all times." Some may suggest that the propaganda campaign that I speak of is a farce; I would beg to differ.

Final Thoughts

In July 2014, my family and I traveled to Washington, D.C. for our summer vacation. We spent a week in the nation's capital taking in the various sights and scenes of the city. Perhaps the highlight of our visit was a tour of the White House. My wife had arranged, through our congressman, this "bucket list" experience. We had to submit our names months in advance just to be considered for the tour. We found out that we were selected to participate in the experience just days before we left for D.C. My wife and I specifically wanted our children to place their feet in the White House while under the administration of the country's first African American president. The tour was a self-guided excursion through the East Wing that took all of twenty minutes to complete. In our effort to savor the experience, we paid meticulous attention to every little detail. It was an experience I will never forget. I only hope that my children appreciated the experience as much as I did. I hope they will one day realize the significance of the occasion.

My wife also arranged, through our congressman, a tour of the United States Capitol. This building represents, perhaps more than the White House, the values and principles that undergird America. It is the symbol of democracy, where legislators who often hold opposing views come together in an egalitarian fashion to deliberate the nation's concerns. The tour provided many highlights and amazements. The first that I will mention is the Old Supreme Court Chamber. An aesthetically and architecturally pleasing room, though smaller than I imagined, was the site where the landmark Dred Scott case took place. As we walked through the courtroom, I tried to imagine the space filled with court officials, attorneys and Supreme Court Justices as they "declared that African Americans had never been citizens of the United States."[19]

For sure, the focal point of the building is the Capitol dome. It majestically rises above much of the city's other impressive landmarks. Beneath the dome is the rotunda, the space that is often referred to as the "symbolic and physical heart" of the edifice. It is the room where countless dignitaries have lay in state. The room is awe-inspiring to say the least. Because the domed ceiling extends nearly 200 feet above your head, the space makes one feel quite diminutive. Around the circular room stands several statues, most of past presidents. In my opinion, all of the statues are depicted regally, standing authoritatively erect, with the exception of one, Martin Luther King, Jr. Though I am not certain of the dimensions of Dr. King's bust, his statue is noticeably smaller than the others. As well, the model in my opinion does not capture Dr. King's true essence. The head and eyes of the structure are downcast as if staring at the floor. I was not around when Dr. King was alive. In fact, I didn't come along until three years after his death. However, there have not been any portraits or portrayals that I have seen where Dr. King's countenance is that of dejection. I brought this observation to my wife's attention; we hypothesized that King's model is, perhaps, smaller than the others because he was not a U.S. President. But, we could not come up with a viable reason for the sculpture's crestfallen disposition.

Up along the base of the dome, there is a decorative band (a frieze) that wraps around the entire room. The images in the band depict the so-called founding of America up to the birth of the Wright Brothers' dream of flying. The pictorial takes on a repoussé artistic design, where the images seem to protrude from the wall; the images are striking.

There are no depictions of the African American people who helped to assemble this country and the Capitol building structure itself. There is not even a brief glimpse of America's economic springboard—slavery. I know for sure that enslaved Africans helped to build the structure, yet there exists no portrayal of them in the rendering. Throughout this beautifully arranged room, the alleged center of the United States capital city, the only African American image is that of a downtrodden Martin Luther King, Jr. Is this intentionally done? How can the space that is thought of as the embodiment of America not include a significant portion of its citizenry? There is no secret that African Americans help build this country, yet no reference is made to us in the space that supposedly personifies America. The omission is quite disappointing as well as revealing.

All across the city are monuments dedicated mainly to the country's founding fathers. The three that are arguably most significant to Black America are the Martin Luther King, Jr. Memorial, the Lincoln Memorial and the Jefferson Memorial. We know why King's memorial is important to Black America, however the Lincoln Memorial is significant because of President Lincoln's supposed role in emancipating the Black body in America, and because the steps of the Lincoln Memorial are where Dr. King rendered his iconic "I Have A Dream" speech. The Jefferson Memorial is significant because of Jefferson's many contributions, primarily as the lead author of the Declaration of Independence and 3rd President of the United States of America. Jefferson is a clear-cut example of the puzzling paradox the United States embodied and still embodies: he owned slaves, but often spoke of freedom for all.

As you walk into the Jefferson Memorial, you are immediately struck with awe by the statue of Jefferson himself. It is a towering structure in the middle of a massive, handsomely crafted stone gazebo. After your eyes are drawn away from the captivating figure in the center of the room, you notice the engraved quotations on the walls surrounding the statue. The passage that garnered my lasting attention reads:

"GOD WHO GAVE US LIFE GAVE US LIBERTY. CAN THE LIBERTIES OF A NATION BE SECURE WHEN WE HAVE REMOVED A CONVICTION THAT THESE LIBERTIES

ARE THE GIFT OF GOD? INDEED I TREM-
BLE FOR MY COUNTRY WHEN I REFLECT
THAT GOD IS JUST, THAT HIS JUSTICE
CANNOT SLEEP FOREVER. COMMERCE
BETWEEN MASTER AND SLAVE IS DES-
POTISM. NOTHING IS MORE CERTAIN-
LY WRITTEN IN THE BOOK OF FATE
THAN THAT THESE PEOPLE ARE TO BE
FREE. ESTABLISH THE LAW FOR EDU-
CATING THE COMMON PEOPLE. THIS
IT IS THE BUSINESS OF THE STATE TO
EFFECT AND ON A GENERAL PLAN."

Here, Jefferson seems to wrestle earnestly with his own actions in light of his deeper convictions. He is grappling with the fact that he has played an active role in subjugating an entire race of people. He treads just short of being apologetic toward those who have been systematically denied their God-given rights. Midway through his revelation, he appears to both dread and celebrate the sovereignty of God's judgment all at once. In the end, he declares that the enslaved should be made free. His recommendation of freedom comes with a call to educate.

I highlight Jefferson's thoughts and the other national landmarks in an effort to make more noticeable the conundrum America represents. It is so progressive in so many ways, but just as repressive in other ways. It is, at once, the greatest experiment in democracy and the greatest mockery of it. The account that America shares with the world about its core principles and values contradicts gravely with its deeds and actions.

I draw attention to these past and current facts and figures in an effort to educate. I intend to remind African Americans to think critically before we wholeheartedly accuse our own of being "crabs in a barrel." We must (1) give full consideration to how we landed in the "barrel" in the first place and (2) bear in mind the living conditions once we inhabited the "barrel." As one of my favorite cartoons (G.I. Joe) as a kid proclaimed, "Knowing is half the battle." We must consider the two preceding points as we build our lives together. But knowing is indeed half the battle; the other half must be action. Action, first, to reduce the margins of the so-called barrel and then escape, together, the confines of said barrel. In due course, the barrel's elimination must be our ultimate goal.

Some who read these pages will conclude that I have absolved Black people from any culpability in the overarching matter, that I am blaming all but us for the station we collectively find ourselves. To the contrary, I have and will continue to admonish Black folk to "get up, get out and get something."[20] We cannot afford to sit around, belly-aching about our lot in life. Things are as they are, but we have the abilities to change those things. Part of changing, at times, includes telling the truth about our less-than-productive behaviors. It also includes telling the truth about our country. To be sure, any society whose foundation is rooted in a systemic and systematic subjugation of a particular group of people must be held partially responsible when assessing the progress of the descendants of the formerly subjugated group. Make no mistakes about it, America is culpable, considering that it has effectively convinced many of its citizens to view other citizens as inferior based simply on the color of their skin.

In conclusion, if we (African Americans) are going to continue to compare ourselves to crabs, we must change the phrase in question altogether. As I insinuated in the beginning, I believe that the phrase should be changed to "crabs in a boiling pot." Such a semantic change transforms the meaning of the expression completely. The new idiom implores us to consider the premise under which the phrase is being expressed. If and when we use the phrase "crabs in a boiling pot," we automatically invoke a cognitive understanding that takes into consideration the environment in which "crabs" exist. Crabs cannot and will not survive in a pot of boiling water; neither will humans.

Ultimately, I am suggesting that we stop using the analogy altogether. Crabs in a barrel or pot are trying to survive in an environment that is not intended for their survival. We blame the crabs for acting in a certain way without ever taking into consideration the structures that have placed them in the environment in the first place. Many African Americans, like crabs, are placed into environments that are not conducive for their survival. We must, first, consider these circumstances and then do something to change them. As President Obama often said throughout both his terms, "We are the change we have been looking for." A song performed by one of my favorite hip-hop groups, Outkast, speaks directly to our need to help ourselves:

> "You need to get up, get out and get something
> How will you make it, if you never even try
> You need to get up, get out and get something
> 'Cause you and I got to do for you and I."

DEFINITIONS OF KEY TERMS

1. <u>African American/Black</u> – Used interchangeably throughout the manuscript, pertains to American Blacks of African ancestry, their history and their culture (The American Heritage Dictionary, 1991).

2. <u>Bias/prejudice</u> – An adverse judgment or opinion formed beforehand or without knowledge or examination of the facts (The American Heritage Dictionary, 1991.)

3. <u>Caucasian American/White</u> – Used interchangeably throughout the manuscript, pertains to European descendants now residing in America, who are believed to have originated near the Caucasus Mountains (Cashmore et. al, 1994).

4. <u>Culture</u> – a) The sum total of lived experience; a socialized means of survival that any group of people acquires in response to their lived environment b) The total way of life of a people; the social legacy the individual acquires from his or her group; a way of thinking, feeling and believing. c) A pattern of arrangements, behaviors whereby a society achieves collective achievement (Cashmore et al, 1994).

5. <u>Identity</u> - One component of an individual's overall self-concept that involves the adoption of certain personal attitudes, feelings, characteristics and behaviors (Parham & White, 1990).

6. Power - In relation to race and ethnic relations, power is the ability to exact a degree of compliance or obedience of others in accordance with one's own will (Cashmore et al, 1994).

7. Privilege - A special right, immunity or benefit enjoyed only by a person or group of people beyond the advantages of others (Dictionary.com).

8. Race - A social and political construct used to classify certain ethnic groups (Bennett, 1999). A group of people united or classified together on the basis of common history, nationality or geographical distribution (The American Hertiage Dictionary, 1991).

9. Racial Identity - A sense of group collective identity based on one's perception that he or she shares a common racial heritage with a particular racial group (Bennett, 1999).

10. Racism - A system of advantage base on race (Tatum, 1997).

11. Self-efficacy - An individual's belief about whether they can execute the necessary procedures for success in given situation (Pearson, 2008).

12. Stereotype - An overgeneralization about the behavior or other characteristics of particular groups (Cashmore et al, 1994).

END NOTES

INTRODUCTION

1. a) Long-standing members of a group or party especially ones who are often unwilling to accept change or new ideas. b) A group of established prestige and influence within a larger group. http://www.merriam-webster.com/
2. Joseph C. Phillips, *He Talk Like A White Boy: Reflections on Faith, Family, Politics, and Authencity* (Philadelphia, PA: Running Press, 2006).
3. Jude 1:3 "Dear friends, although I was very eage to write to you about the salvation we share, I felt had to write and urge you to contend for the faith that was once for all entrusted to the saints." The New International Version Bible
4. Martin L. King, Jr., *Where Do We Go From Here: Chaos or Community?* (Boston, MA: Beacon Press, 1968).

CHAPTER ONE

1. Arguably the most significant phrase from the U.S. Declaration of Independence, often referred to as the "immortal declaration".

2. In August of 1619, the first (20) indentured Africans were exchanged for food on the banks of the James River in Jamestown, Virginia. Lerone Bennett, Jr., *The Shaping of Black America* (New York, NY: Penguin Books, 1993).

3. Samuel H. Williamson and Louis P. Cain "Measuring Slavery in 2011 Dollars*" *Measuring Worth,* (2015) URL: http://www.measuringworth.org/slavery.php

4. Sven Beckert, *Empire of Cotton: A Global History* (New York, NY: Borzoi Books, Alfred Knopf Publishing, 2014).

5. Craig Steven Wilder, "A Story That Was Too Ugly to Tell" The Chronicle Review, (September 27, 2013).

6. Ibid #4

7. "Slavery on South Carolina Rice Plantations: The Migration of People and Knowledge in Early Colonial America" URL http://www.ricediversity.org/outreach/educattorscorner/documents/Carolina-Gold-Stdent-handout.pdf

8. Ibid #3

9. Julia Floyd Smith, *Slavery and Rice Culture in Low Country Georgia, 1750 – 1860* (Knoxville, TN: The University of Tennessee Press, 1985).

10. Anthony Gene Carey, *Sold Down the River: Slavery in the Lower Chattahoochee Valley of Alabama and Georgia* (Tuscaloosa, AL: The University of Alabama Press, 2011).

11. Ashley C. Allen, "The 10 richest U.S. presidents," USA Today, (February 17, 2014). URL http://www.usatoday.com/story/money/business/2014/02/15/10-richest-presidents/5514567/

12. Lacy Ford, *Deliver Us from Evil: The Slavery Question in the Old South* (New York, NY: Oxford University Press, 2009).

13. Ibid

14. Joy DeGruy Leary, *Post Traumatic Slave Syndrome: America's Legacy of Enduring Injury and Healing* (Milwaukie, OR: Uptone Press, 2005).

15. Robert Bernasconi and Tommy Lee Lott, *The Idea of Race*, (Indianapolis, IN: Hackett Publishing Company, Inc., 2000).

16. Nell Irvin Painter, "Why White People Are Called 'Caucasian?" *Collective Degradation: Slavery and the Constitution of Race*, 5th Annual Gilder Lehrman Center International Conference at Yale University, (November 7-8. 2003). URL http://www.yale.edu/glc/events/race/Painter.pdf

17. Ibid #13

18.   Jason Ziedenberg and Vincent Schiraldi, "Cellblocks or Classrooms? The Funding of Higher Education and Corrections and Its Impacts on African American Men" *Justice Policy Institute,* (September 2002). URL http://www.justicepolicy.org/uploads/justice policy/documents/02-09_rep_cellblocksclassrooms _bb-ac.pdf

19.   Jo Jones and William D. Mosher, "Fathers' Involvement with Their Children: United States, 2006-2010" *National Health Statistics Reports,* Number 71, Center for Disease Control, (December 20, 2013). URL http://www.cdc.gov/nchs/data/nhsr/nhsr071.pdf

20.   Signithia Fordham and John Uzo Ogbu, "Black Students' School Success: Coping with the 'Burden of Acting White'" *National Institute of Education,* Annual Meeting of the American Anthropological Association, (December 3-7), 1985. URL http://files.eric.ed.gov/fulltext/ED281948.pdf

21.   Roland Fryer, "Acting White: A Social Price Paid by the Best and Brightest Minority Students" *Education Next,* Volume 6, Number 1, (Winter 2006), pg. 52-59. URL http://educationnext.org/actingwhite/

22.   Beverly Daniel Tatum, *Why Are All the Black Kids Sitting Together in the Cafeteria? : And Other Conversations About Race* (New York, NY: Basic Books, 1997).

23. Karolyn Tyson, William Darity, Jr and Domini R. Castellino, "It's Not A Black Thing: Understanding the Burden of Acting White and Other Dilemmas of High Achievement" *American Sociological Review*, Volume 70, Number 4, (August 2005), pg. 582-605 URL http://www.jstor.org/stable /4145378

24. Ibid #20

25. Edward Rhymes, "Acting White: African-American Students and Education" *The Black Commentator*, Issue 100, (July 22, 2004). URL http://www.black commentator.com/100/100 cover acting white pdf. html

26. John Uzo Ogbu and Herbert Simons, "Voluntary and Involuntary Minorities: A Cultural-Ecological Theory of School Performance with Some Implications for Education" *Anthropology & Education Quarterly*, Volume 29, Issue 2, (June 1998), pg. 155 -264. URL http://eric.ed.gov/?id=EJ576651

CHAPTER TWO

1. Chris Crothers, "Black Male: Why the Mid-South Cannot Afford to Ignore the Disparities Facing Its Black Men and Boys" *Foundation for the Mid-South,* 2008. URL http://www.fndmidsouth.org/sites/default/files/ Black Male web.pdf

2. "Given Half A Chance: The Schott 50 State Report on Public Education and Black Males" *The Schott Foundation for Public Education*, (2008). URL http://www.schottfoundation.org/drupal/docs/ schott50statereport-execsummary.pdf

3. Raymond Winbush, *The Warrior Method: A Program for Rearing Healthy Black Boys.* (New York, NY: HarperCollins Books, 2001).

4. Ibid #1

5. National Urban League, *The State of Black America 2007: Portrait of the Black Male.* (New York, NY: The Beckham Publishing Group, Inc., 2007).

6. Ibid #5

7. Ivory Toldson, "Breaking Barriers: Plotting the Path to Academic Success for School Age African American Males," *Congressional Black Caucus Foundation, Inc.,* (2008). URL http://cdm16064. contentdm.oclc.org/cdm/ref/collection/ p266901coll4/id/2279

8. Randolph G. Potts, "Emancipatory Education Versus School-Based Prevention in African American Communities" *American Journal of Community Psychology,* Volume 31, Numbers 1 &2, (March 2003). URL http://kemetrise.sytes.net: 8245/Kemetrise%20Library/emancipatoryeducation. pdf

9. Ibid #7

10. Marcus Rediker, T*he Slave Ship: A Human History.* (New York, NY: Viking Penguin Group, 2007).

11. Earl Ofari Hutchinson, *The Assassination of the Black Male Image.* (New York, NY: A Touchstone Book, 1994).

12. Margaret Talbot, "Matters of Privacy" *The New Yorker,* (October 6, 2014). URL http://www.newyorker.com/magazine/2014/10/06/matters-privacy

13. Ibid #12

14. John Lauinger, "NASCAR champion Tony Stewart hits, kills driver in upstate N.Y. dirt-track race," *New York Daily News,* (August, 10, 2014). URL http://www.nydailynews.com/sports/more-sports/nascar-champion-tony-stewart-hits-driver-reports-article-1.1898395

15. Madison Hartman, "Tony Stewart had long history of aggressive racing style before accident that killed Kevin Ward, Jr." *New York Daily News,* (August 11, 2014). URL http://www.nydailynews.com/sports/more-sports/tony-stewart-long-history-aggressive-racing-style-accident-killed-kevin-ward-jr-article-1.1899676

16. "Autopsy Report for Michael Brown" *St. Louis Post-Dispatch,* (October 21, 2014). URL http://www.stltoday.com/online/pdf-autopsy-report-for-michael-brown/pdf_ce018d0c-5998-11e4-b700-001a4bcf6878.html

17. Taylor Wofford, "What We Learned from an Independent Autopsy of Michael Brown" *Newsweek,* (August, 18, 2014). URL http://www.newsweek.com/what-we-learned-michael-browns-autopsy-265247

18. keepemhonest, "Autopsy suggests Mike Brown DID have arms in 'surrender' pose when Darren Wilson killed him" *Daily KOS*, (August, 18, 2014). URL http://www.dailykos.com/story/2014/08/18/1322540/-Autopsy-suggests-Mike-Brown-had-his-arms-in-surrender-position-when-Darren-Wilson-killed-him#

19. Frank Vyan Walton, "Pathologist Dr. Cyril Wecht reacts to 'absurd' defense of Darren Wilson" *Daily KOS*, (November 29, 2014). URL http://www.dailykos.com/story/2014/11/29/1348243/-Pathologist-Dr-Cyril-Wecht-Reacts-to-Absurd-Defense-of-Darren-Wilson

20. Ibid #10

21. Reference to Billie Holiday's song "Strange Fruit" which addresses the lynching of African Americans in Southern states, mainly during the Jim Crow era.

22. U.S. Department of Justice Civil Rights Division, *Investigation of the Ferguson Police Department*, (March 4, 2015). URL http://www.justice.gov/sites/default/files/opa/press-releases/attachments/2015/03/04/ferguson_police_department_report.pdf

23. Mike Prada, "Lebron James Event Raises $6 Million In Ad Sales, $2.5 Million For Boys and Girls Club" *SB Nation*, (July 8, 2010). URL http://www.sbnation.com/2010/7/8/1559877/lebron-james-free-agent-espn-event-ad-sales

24. Bill Rhoden, *Forty Million Dollar Slaves: The Rise, Fall and Redemption of the Black Athlete.* (New York, NY: Three Rivers Press, 2006).

25. Rich Thomaselli, "All The King's Men: The LeBron James Version of Entourage" *Advertising Age,* (July 17, 2006). URL http://adage.com/article/news/king-s-men-lebron-james-version-entourage/110516/

26. Elena Bergeron, "Very Smart Player" *ESPN.com,* (October 18, 2013). URL http://espn.go.com/nba/story/_/id/9840201/lebron-james-most-powerful-active-athlete-entrepreneur-sports-espn-magazine

27. Adam Epstein, "All the ways Mayweather-Pacquiao will be the biggest boxing match ever" *QUARTZ,* (February 24, 2015). URL http://qz.com/349274/all-the-ways-mayweather-pacquiao-will-be-the-biggest-boxing-match-ever/

28. Ibid #27

29. Walter Dean Myers, *The Greatest: Muhammad Ali* (New York, NY: Scholastic, Inc., 2001).

30. Jordan Goodman, *Paul Robeson: A Watch Man* (Brooklyn, NY: Verso, 2013).

31. Adrian Sheppe, "James Baldwin's Discovery of Self" *Americans in Paris,* (Fall 2010). URL https://uramericansinparis.wordpress.com/2010/12/08/james-baldwins-discovery-of-self/

32. "W.E.B. Du Bois Biography," *Biography.com. A&E Network* URL http://www.biography.com/people/web-du-bois-9279924

33. Ibid #32

34. Bob Greene, *Hang Time: Days and Dreams with Michael Jordan.* (New York, NY: St. Martin's Paperbacks, 1993).

35.   Howard Gardner, *Frames of Mind: The Theory of Multiple Intelligences.* (New York, NY: Basic Books, 1993).

36.   Ben Watanabe, "Youth Football League Bars 11-Year-Old Prodigy From Scoring Touchdowns" *NESN.com,* (October 2, 2011). URL http://nesn.com/2011/10/youth-football-league-bars-11-year-old-prodigy-from-scoring-touchdowns/

37.   Benjamin S. Bloom, T*axonomy of Educational Objectives Book 1: Cognitive Domain.* (White Plains, NY: Longman, 1984).

38.   Michelle Alexander, *The New Jim Crow: Mass Incarceration in the Age of Colorblindness.* (New York, NY: The New Press, 2010)

CHAPTER THREE

1.   "Race and the Criminal Justice System in the United States 2013" The Sentencing Project. URL http://sentencingproject.org/doc/publications/rd_ICCPR%20Race%20and%20Justice%20Shadow%20Report.pdf

2.   Michelle Alexander, *The New Jim Crow: Mass Incarceration in the Age of Colorblindness.* (New York, NY: The New Press, 2010)

3.   "Crime in the United States 2012" *Federal Bureau of Investigation (FBI),* Criminal Justice Information Services Division. URL https://www.fbi.gov/about-us/cjis/ucr/crime-in-the-u.s/2012/crime-in-the-u.s.-2012/persons-arrested

4. "2013 Annual Report: Missouri Vehicle Stops" Missouri Attorney General Office. URL https://www.ago.mo.gov/home/vehicle-stops-report/2013-executive-summary

5. Kelly Welch, "Black Criminal Stereotypes and Racial Profiling" *Journal of Contemporary Criminal Justice*, Volume 23, Number 2, (August 2007), pg. 276-288. URL http://www.sagepub.com/gabbidonstudy/articles/Welch.pdf

6. Ted Chiricos, Kelly Welch and Marc Gertz, "Racial Typification of Crime and Support for Punitive Measures" *CRIMINOLOGY,* Volume 43, Number 2, (2004). URL http://onlinelibrary.wiley.com/doi/10.1111/j.1745-9125.2004.tb00523.x/pdf

7. Frances Henry, Patricia Hastings, and Brian Freer, "Perceptions of race and crime in Ontario: Empirical evidence from Toronto and the Durham region" *Canadian Journal of Criminology,* (October 1996), pg. 469-476. URL http://heinonline.org/HOL/Page?handle=hein.journals/cjccj38&div=39&g_sent=1&collection=journals

8. Abraham H. Foxman and John Marttilla, "Quantifying Campus Racism" *Washington Post,* (August 18, 1993). URL http://www.washingtonpost.com/archive/opinions/1993/08/18/quantifying-campus-racism/74ab5a23-e40d-4b0a-adcb-59ab3e7677c4/

9.   Kimberly Papillon, "The Hard Science of Civil
       Rights: How Neuroscience Changes the
       Conversation" *Equal Justice Society.* URL
       http://equaljusticesociety.org/law/implicitbias/
       primer/
10.   Paul Kivel, "Culture of Power" *What Makes Racial
       Diversity Work in Higher Education: Academic
       Leaders Present Successful Policies and Strategies.*
       (Sterling, VA: Stylus Publishing, 2004).
11.   Peter Heinze, "Let's Talk About Race, Baby" *Multi-
       cultural Education,* (Fall 2008). URL
       http://files.eric.ed.gov/fulltext/EJ822393.pdf
12.   Beverly Daniel Tatum, *Why Are All the Black Kids
       Sitting Together in the Cafeteria? And Other
       Conversations About Race* (New York, NY:
       Basic Books, 1997).
13.   Tim Wise, *White Like Me: Reflections on Race from
       a Privileged Son* (Berkeley, CA: Soft Skull Press,
       2005).
14.   Ibid #1
15.   Ibid #10
16.   Peter Heinze, "Why White People Love White Su-
       premacists: A Psychoanalytic Group Relations
       Perspective of White Anti-Racism" *The Whiteness
       Papers,* Number 5, (April 2006). URL
       http://www.researchgate.net/profile/Peter_Heinze/
       publication/237145287_Why_White_People_Love_
       White_Supremacists_A_psychoanalytic_group_
       relations_perspective_of_white_anti-racism/
       links/0046351b914cd1ef08000000.pdf

17.   Ibid #12
18.   The Drug Policy Alliance (DPA), "A Brief History of the Drug War". URL http://www.drugpolicy.org/new-solutions-drug-policy/brief-history-drug-war
19.   Katheryn Russell-Brown, *The Color of Crime, 2nd Edition.* (New York, NY: New York University Press, 2009).
20.   William E. Cross, *Shades of Black: Diversity in African American Identity.* (Philadelphia, PA: Temple University Press, 1991).

CHAPTER FOUR

1.   Rakesh Kochhar and Richard Fry, "Wealth inequality has widened along racial, ethnic lines since end of Great Recession" *Pew Research Center* (December 12, 2014). URL http://www.pewresearch.org/fact-tank/2014/12/12/racial-wealth-gaps-great-recession/
2.   Louis L. Woods, II, "The Federal Home Loan Bank Board, Redlining, and the National Proliferation of Racial Lending Discrimination, 1921-1950," *Journal of Urban History,* Volume 38, Issue 6, (November 2012), pg. 1036-1059. URL http://juh.sagepub.com/content/38/6/1036.full.pdf+html
3.   Ibid #2

4.   Ira Katznelson, *When Affirmative Action was White: An Untold History of Racial Inequality in Twentieth-Century America.* (New York, NY: W.W. Norton & Company, 2005).

5.   Sherman L. Richards and George M. Blackburn, "A Demographic History of Slavery: Georgetown County, South Carolina, 1850," *The South Carolina Historical Magazine,* Volume 76, No. 4, (October 1975) pg. 215-224. URL http://www.jstor.org/stable/27567334?seq=1# page_scan_tab_contents

6.   Paul Taylor and D'Vera Cohn, "A Milestone En Route to a Majority Minority Nation." Pew Research Center, (November 7, 2012). URL http://www.pewsocialtrends.org/2012/11/07/ a-milestone-en-route-to-a-majority-minority- nation/

7.   John Hope Bryant, *How the Poor Can Save Capitalism: Rebuilding the Path to the Middle Class* (San Francisco, CA: Berrett-Koehler Publishers, 2014).

8.   Ibid #7

9.   Steve Suitts, Vanessa Elkan, and Dorian Woolaston, "A New Diverse Majority: Students of Color in the South's Public Schools, 2010" SEF Research Report, *The Southern Education Foundation,* (2010). URL http://www.southerneducation.org/getattachment/ 884678f3-ca14-474f-a5e4-be2fa687136c/2010- A-New-Diverse-Majority-Students-of-Color-in- t.aspx

10. Maya Kalyanpur and Beth Harry, *Cultural Reciproc ity in Special Education: Building Family-Professional Relationships* (Baltimore, MD: Paul H. Brookes Publishing, 2012).

11. Samuel Betances "How to Become an Outstanding Educator of Hispanic and African-American First-Generation College Students" *What Makes Racial Diversity Work in Higher Education: Academic Leaders Present Successful Policies and Strategies.* (Sterling, VA: Stylus Publishing, 2004).

12. Ibid #11

13. Ibid #6

14. Ibid #11

15. Ibid #4

16. Ibid #4

17. Thomas Shapiro, Tatjana Meschede, and Sam Osoro, "The Roots of the Widening Racial Wealth Gap: Explaining the Black-White Economic Divide," Institute on Assets and Social Policy, (February 2013). URL http://community-wealth.org/content/roots-widening-racial-wealth-gap-explaining-black-white-economic-divide

CHAPTER FIVE

1. Marcus Rediker, *The Slave Ship: A Human History.* (New York, NY: Viking Penguin Group, 2007).

2. Reference to Langston Hughes' Poem, "Mother to Son" (1922).

3.   Online Etymology Dictionary. URL
      http://www.etymonline.com/index.php?term=
      inspire
4.   Genesis 2:7, "God formed Man out of dirt from the
      ground and blew into his nostrils the breath of life.
      The Man came alive - a living soul." The Holy Bible,
      New International Version.
5.   James 2:17, "In the same way, faith by itself, if it is
      not accompanied by action, is dead." The Holy Bible,
      New International Version.
6.   Ralph Ellison, *Invisible Man.* (New York, NY:
      Vintage Books, 1995).
7.   Randall Robinson, *The Debt: What America Owes
      to Blacks.* (New York, NY: Penguin Books, 2001).
8.   A spin-off of Marcus Garvey's quote, "Up, you
      mighty race! You can accomplish what you will."
9.   Shane Lopez, *Making Hope Happen: Create the
      Future You Want for Yourself and Others.*
      (New York, NY: Atria Paperback, 2013).
10.   Robert A. Emmons, T*hanks! How Practicing Grati-
      tude Can Make You Happier.*
      (New York, NY: Houghton Mifflin Paperback, 2008).
11.   Earl Shorris, "As a weapon in the hands of the rest
      less poor," *Harper Magazine,* (September 1997).
      URL http://www.harpers.org/archive/1997/09/
      0074349
12.   Ibid #10
13.   Bob and Judy Fisher, *Life is a Gift: Inspiration from
      the Soon Departed.* (New York, NY:FaithWords,
      2008).

14. Steve Perry, *Man Up: Nobody is Coming to Save Us.* (Hartford, CT: Renegade Books, 2006).

15. Reference to William Ernest Henley's Poem "Invictus" (1875).

16. Kevin Johnson, Meghan Hoyer and Brad Heath, "Local Police involved in 400 killings per year," *USA Today,* (August 15, 2014). URL http://www.usatoday.com/story/news/nation/2014/08/14/police-killings-data/14060357/

17. Malcom Gladwell, *The Tipping Point: How Little Things Can Make a Big Difference.* (New York, NY: First Back Bay Paperback, 2002).

18. Ryan Gabrielson, Ryann Grochowski Jones and Eric Sagara, "Deadly Force, in Black and White," *ProPublica,* (October 10, 2014). URL http://www.propublica.org/article/deadly-force-in-black-and-white

19. The majority opinion delivered by Chief Justice Roger Taney in the 1857 Dred Scott Case, argued that persons of African descent could not be, nor ever were intended to be, U.S. citizens, according to the United States Constitution.

20. Reference to a song by rap duo Outkast featuring Goodie Mob, "Git Up Git Out," (1994).

Dr. Rodney D. Smith is the Associate Director in the International Center for Supplemental Instruction at the University of Missouri-Kansas City. He also serves as an Adjunct Professor in the School of Education and the founding advisor for the Men of Color Campus Initiative. Dr. Smith's career in education spans 20+ years, where his scholarly interests have focused on educational leadership and administration, African American male student achievement, culturally reciprocative pedagogy, diversity & inclusion, and urban education. Dr. Smith holds a Doctor of Education Degree from Tennessee State University and a Bachelor of Arts Degree from Morris Brown College. He is married to Stephenie K. Smith and they are the proud parents of two wonderful children.

CPSIA information can be obtained
at www.ICGtesting.com
Printed in the USA
LVOW12s1100281016

510701LV00001B/14/P